A PARENT'S GUIDE TO THE GAP YEAR

ANDREA WIEN

GAP TO GREAT

First published in the United States in 2015 by

OnAviator, LLC

Gap to Great

www.gaptogreat.com

www.andreawien.com

© Andrea Wien 2015

Author: Wien, Andrea, 1985-

Title: Gap to great : a parent's guide to the gap year /

Andrea Wien.

ISBN: 978-0-9944129-0-4 (pbk.)

Subjects: Gap years; Education; Parenting; Experiences; Success;

Life lessons; Self-actualization, Self-awareness; Individuation

Cover Design by Karla Sanders

Interior Design by Vanessa Maynard

Author photo by Jason Malouin

Printed in America by OnAviator

10 9 8 7 6 5 4 3 2 1

For Matt, my biggest supporter and the one who always reminds me to keep smiling, even when I don't want to.

CONTENTS

INTRODUCTION

In his TED Talk, author and speaker Mark Lindquist says the most uninformed decision we'll ever make is when we're forced to choose our college major.

Think about it: before we've even had to do our own laundry, we're expected to decide what we want to do every day for the rest of our lives.

Seems a little backwards, doesn't it?

Today, 72% of the American workforce is disengaged from their jobs. To put it simply, the traditional system isn't working. Instead, it's forcing people into degrees that lead to mounds of student loan debt, unfulfilling careers, and high levels of unnecessary stress and frustration. Going to college, taking on an internship, and heading straight into a job post-graduation no longer provide a guaranteed route to career success and happiness. Something is clearly broken. When did the "sure bet" of attending higher education to secure a cushy career turn into a risky game of chance?

We send our kids directly into college after high school, worried that if they take time off from formal education they may lose their direction and drive to succeed. At the same time, we're seeing a sharp increase in the number of students on antidepressant and anti-anxiety medications. Thirty-two percent of college students in a recent American College Health Association study reported feeling "so depressed that it was difficult to function" at some point in the last year, and more than 50% felt overwhelming anxiety, making academic success a challenge.

College tuition rates have gone through the roof—up 50% since 2000—while job satisfaction rates have plummeted. The national student loan debt now hovers at a staggering $1.2 *trillion*, an increase of 84% since the 2008 recession.

And for what? We're no happier once we graduate college and head out to the workforce. If anything, our pesky persistence to drive kids through the system is creating students and adults who are overstressed, overworked, and—frankly—over it.

Like many of my friends, I did everything right. In high school, I was editor of the student newspaper. I volunteered, played basketball, studied enough, and even interned with a news station at the local college. I wrote college essays that landed me acceptance at schools around America and gained early admission at one of the top journalism programs in the country.

But when I started college in the fall of 2004, I still had no idea what I wanted to do. "You've always been a good writer," my dad nudged. Because I also loved sports, I settled on broadcast journalism and quickly set to work taking classes that would turn me into an NFL sideline reporter. It wasn't until halfway through my sophomore year that anyone thought it might be a good idea to tell me what it actually took to make my dream a reality.

Years of working in a small market covering Little League championships before I'd even be considered for work in a big city? That didn't sound appealing. I wanted to move to New York. I wanted to make a difference. And I wanted to do it now.

At the time, I was working to pay my way through college as a part-time wedding videographer when my boss brought up a major in public relations. His sister worked in PR, and he suggested that entering that field would allow me to jump in, move up, and start doing interesting work right away. It seemed like a no-brainer. I swapped focus and hit the ground running.

Then came my junior year. I landed my dream internship that summer in NYC, working in fashion PR and planning events like the MAXIM Hot 100 Party. The dream lasted approximately two hours before I realized that PR was not my calling.

When I went back to school that fall, I weighed my options. Should I switch majors again, which would add more time to my college career, not to mention my rapidly growing bundle of student loan debt? Not a chance. I'd put in too much time, energy, and money to start over, so I stuck with it, earned my degree, and set off to make a name for myself.

Soon the bills were piling up, and I clung tightly to the first job that offered me a paycheck. Because my degree and my internship were both in PR, I took a job working at a prestigious international firm, but I hated every minute of it.

As the months ticked by, the vicious cycle of working just to make ends meet kicked into high gear. Suddenly I had a whole adult life, but with none of the perks I'd imagined. The concept of doing something else seemed like a distant pipe dream. How could I possibly explore other career options when I could barely afford to pay off loans, eat, and make rent?

By the time I turned twenty-four, I was burnt out. I quit my job, threw my belongings into storage, and took off for a four-month tour of Europe. At the end of my trip, my credit cards were maxed out, I had no job, no apartment, and still no idea of what to do next. During a fourteen-hour layover at JFK on the way back to my parent's house in Ohio, I slept in the airport because I couldn't afford the twelve-dollar train fare into the city to stay with friends.

In short, things weren't looking too great. I decided maybe a change of scenery would help, and with my boyfriend at the time in tow, I drove across the country to Seattle where I spent my time pitching travel and food stories to editors. The upside? Editors were interested in my writing. The downside? None of them wanted to pay me.

Now, you don't have to have a degree in economics to know that money going out without more money coming in isn't exactly the recipe for success. I'd hit another dead end. When I reached the end of my rope on the West Coast, I went back to New York and reluctantly took a job working for a digital agency in SoHo.

By the time I turned twenty-eight, I was fed up. My peers and I sat around at dinner parties complaining about our jobs, griping about our bosses, and asking the same question: how did we all get here? When I started thinking more deeply about it, I realized it wasn't directly my fault that I didn't know how to identify my passion and pick the right career. The system itself was–and still is—flawed. Schools teach us what they think we need to learn, but not necessarily *how* to learn. Or, to take it a step further, how to learn about ourselves. As memory trainer Jim Kwik says, "There are no classes on how to think, how to be creative, how to focus, how to solve problems, how to read faster, how to remember things."

I became obsessed with why there wasn't a better way, and intrigued by the thought of what might happen if students had the opportunity to step off the treadmill. What would our culture look like if we encouraged young people to explore the world, or to have a profound life experience, before they dedicated countless hours and resources to earning a degree they may barely use?

I began researching programs that would allow young people to hit pause before launching right into the high-pressure world of post-secondary education. I wanted to know if anything existed that would give students this clarity, and if temporarily "opting out" would harm their future success. It's in that research that I discovered the gap year. A concept born in the U.K., this is a period of time that can be filled with transformation and learning about oneself and the world. It can also help create a clearer sense of direction and meaning for students.

WHAT IS A GAP YEAR?

Though the definition of a gap year varies depending on whom you ask, I think the American Gap Association (AGA), a non-profit accreditation and standards-setting organization for gap years, defines it well: "A gap year is an experiential semester or year 'on,' typically taken between high school and college, in order to deepen practical, professional, and personal awareness."

Kathy Cheng, Director of USA Gap Year Fairs and Director of Admissions at the gap year program Dynamy, defines the gap year as an *intentional* period of time between completing high school and beginning college when a student takes steps outside of the traditional classroom experience. "The word 'intentional' is important because you don't haphazardly fall into a gap year," she says. "It's a time to explore the world, reflect on personal values and goals, and prepare to take the next purposeful step in life."

Even with these definitions, however, there's still plenty of room for interpretation. The first confusing bit is that many young people who take a gap year aren't always gone for a full year. At the Center for Interim Programs, the first and longest-running independent gap year counseling organization in the country, counselors choose to call it "gap time" rather than "gap year." So how long does one need to hit pause to differentiate between a gap year and an extended vacation?

"When we're looking at high school and college students who are transitioning from adolescence into adulthood, I think there has to be a longer period of time—at a minimum one to three months—to really deepen the level of experience and to help foster reflection," says Jason Sarouhan, Interim's vice president.

Sarouhan says that's because when students are in an experience for a shorter length of time, it's easy enough to bolster themselves against the adversity, see the light at the end of the tunnel, and muscle their way though any hardship. "Some of the greatest learning comes from having to be resilient within an experience, and to have a range of emotions come through—everything from elation and joy, to frustration and boredom. A gap year is about seeing yourself more fully, and that requires time and direct engagement," he explains.

The definition of a gap year isn't only muddied by time. The activities and experiences that take place during a gap year also vary widely. In the case of a gap year program, students sign on to join a structured, and often supervised, set of activities that takes them through a pre-determined itinerary. On a program, they're also often—though not always—with peers of a similar age. On the other hand, a self-directed gap year—one that's independent of a program—is bound only by the time and geographical restrictions set by the family.

Further complicating the definition is the fact that in many cases, students may choose to do part of their year with a program before opting to travel, volunteer, or work independently. There's no right or wrong in this decision—it's ultimately about the maturity, interests, and comfort level of the students and their families.

Throughout this book, you'll notice that many of the

students I feature opted to go overseas during their time off. While I personally believe there are strong benefits to international travel, including breaking out of one's comfort zone and acclimating to a new culture, it's not imperative that a gap year happen overseas. Plenty of students stay in their home countries—and even their hometowns—during their gap year.

As you read, you'll encounter the opinions of educators, parents, and students regarding what kind of gap year is best. But remember that, when all is said and done, the best gap year is the one that fits the particular student taking it.

To give you a better idea of what different gap years can look like, here are some examples:

- *A three-month, international travel excursion with a structured gap year program*

- *A nine-month trek through India and Nepal with a best friend*

- *Three-months working in a part-time job close to home, three-months volunteering at an orphanage in Peru, three-months living with a homestead family while scuba diving in Australia*

- *A year in the Peace Corps*

- *A six-month hostel hop around Europe*

- *A year interning at three different companies*

- *Seven months teaching English in Ethiopia*

- *Five months cutting down invasive plant species in Louisiana*

Though gap years are varied, individualized experiences, with plenty of room for options, they do share one common thread: they expose students to something they wouldn't get from classroom learning. In a later chapter, we'll discuss how to find the program, or design the gap year, that may be right for your son or daughter.

MAKING A CLEAR DISTINCTION

While a gap year can take many different forms, that's not to say all gap years are equally valuable. There's a world of difference between a well-planned, productive gap year and a twelve-month booze fest. To help differentiate between the two, some colleges and programs choose to call the experiences they offer "bridge years" instead of "gap years."

One program that uses the bridge-year language is Global Citizen Year. Their website explains why:

*"Why do we use the term **"bridge year"** instead of the more traditional term **"gap year"**? The gap year is*

often perceived as a luxury reserved for privileged kids, or those who are somehow "off-track." In contrast, the notion of a bridge year conveys an intentional transition from one life stage to the next. Crossing a bridge is a better metaphor than falling into a gap; and, with the right design, the bridge becomes a launching pad for a lifetime of leadership."

The Tufts 1+4 program also prefers to use the term "bridge year." Mindy Nierenberg, Senior Director of Tisch College Programs at Tufts University and the designer of Tufts' 1+4 Gap Year Program, notes: "A bridge year is any program that is building upon what a student learned in high school, and then encouraging them to make connections in terms of how the year affects their college education, and even the future after that."

I agree that "bridge year" more accurately describes the type of experience I'll discuss in this book, but because the phrase "gap year" is more widely used and recognized, I'll refer to it as such throughout the text.

One further note before we continue: as you move about your research on gap years, you may notice that some organizations capitalize "Gap Year." There's a movement currently to turn "gap year" into a proper noun so that it has a defined meaning. The intention behind this is to suggest that when a gap year is done well, certain components are involved that maximize the chances for growth. While I respect this movement and the push to formalize the term, I've chosen to leave "gap year" lowercased throughout this book.

HOW TO GET THE MOST OUT OF THIS BOOK

This book will introduce you to the world of the gap year between high school and college. By unpacking the common concerns parents have about the gap year journey, we'll shine a light on the unknowns and also delve into what it's like to be a teenager in today's always-on, constantly shifting world. I'll continue to share more about my personal journey with you and give tips and conversation starters to kick-start discussions about the future with your child.

All parents want what's best for their children, but in today's world, it's become more and more difficult to identify what that looks like. I hope that as you read, you'll find useful information that will help you to guide your son or daughter into a confident decision about what comes next.

Because each chapter deals with a different area of the gap year process, it's okay to jump around as you read. Whether you're just hearing about gap years for the first time, or you're trying to familiarize yourself with the concept because your child has chosen to take a gap year, this book will offer reassurance, information, and advice for any stage of the journey.

1: DIRECTING THE APPLE'S FALL FROM THE TREE

"We have a name for it: transitional stress. Even if it's good, it's challenging. It's a time of risk. How are you going to navigate those changes from adolescence to young adulthood?"

– Tara Fass, Los Angeles-based family therapist

The world has changed since you were in high school. Your child is growing up in an interconnected world that's less forgiving in nearly every way. A world where stupid mistakes made in a friend's basement can live forever on the Internet, and an incriminating photo can spread like wildfire through a tiny screen.

Along with the pressure to perform in school, life outside the classroom is a tangled web of sports practices, social media updates, terrorism threats, language-learning lessons, unrelenting bullies, SAT tutors, and smartphones. At the same time, your child is also tasked with "figuring it out" as quickly as possible. In the past, "figuring it out" consisted of choosing a good college, landing an entry-level job, and working your way up the corporate ladder. But now, "figuring it out" is a much taller order.

It's no longer realistic to think that current college grads will find a company, stick with it for thirty years, and retire with a pension when they hit sixty-five. And contrary to common belief, that's not because Millennials—those born between 1980 and the mid-2000s—don't value job security. They do. It's simply that they're less likely than generations before them to stay in a job that doesn't speak to their concept of a higher purpose.

Where some past generations sucked it up in an effort to climb the ranks, this new wave of workers values more than the corner office with a view and a steady paycheck. Gen X kept clear divisions between work and play, while Millennials are flipping that paradigm on its head. To us Millennials, work is play, and vice versa.

Here's how non-Millennial John Brandon explains it in his Inc.com article, "Here's Why Your Definition of Work is Driving Millennials Nuts": "We [parents of Millennials] see work as defined by a place, a time, an org chart, a paycheck, and a boss. It's ingrained in us. For younger people, though, it can be hard to say when work ends and the fun begins. Or maybe the 'fun' is work. Or work and fun mean the exact same thing... Work has flowed into life. It has co-mingled."

Why is this the case? For one, we're kids who have been told our whole lives that we can do anything, be anything, and have it all. Instead of being directed to find a career just to pay the bills, we were also told to hunt down our *true passion*. "Do what you love and love what you do" became the slogan du jour.

The problem is that our parents didn't really believe it. Or if they did, they didn't think our "anything" would be much different than theirs. And so, when we set out to change the tides, to go after something bigger and bolder, to make work a meaningful part of life instead of a means to an end, we were met with disapproval. It wasn't acceptable to make a living as a musician, head out to travel the world, or string together a series of freelance clients.

Just as in generations past, my graduating class saw plenty of doctors, lawyers, accountants, and marketing managers. The difference was that instead of finding satisfaction in the roles we'd assumed, we found ourselves unfulfilled. The shiny dream of career bliss faded quickly.

Even after all of the rah-rah cheerleading of our youth, older Millennials found ourselves in the same cubicles as our parents, staring down an eight-hour workday and holding out for our two weeks of vacation time. We felt cheated, but even more than that, we felt like failures.

The "do what you love" message our parents imparted had merit, but it's close to impossible to teach something you haven't personally experienced. For the vast majority of parents today, fully following a passion was rarely an option, which makes it difficult for them to guide their children down a path they haven't traversed themselves. In a world where it seems like it's getting scarier and harder to raise healthy kids, the default is to fall back on what you know: college + career = security. The somewhat mis-intentioned message of discovering what you love is still as strong as ever, but the method of how to find it is in serious disarray.

I'm a firm believer that people can support themselves doing just about anything if they find a niche and work hard. The problem is that too few people know how to identify their passion and purpose, which can lead to feelings of resentment and despair in adolescence and early adulthood.

"Most parents don't want to hurt their kids; most parents want to do what's best for their kids. And it's quite common to want their children to have economic stability and to secure their economic future. At times, parents impose their own ideas about the jobs they believe will provide that stability," says Karen Bridbord, an individual/couples/and organizational psychologist in New York City.

IQ VERSUS EQ

To find one's passion, one first must find oneself as an individual. Individuation, or the process of distinguishing yourself as different from others, isn't a hard concept to understand, though it can be incredibly difficult for most parents to encourage in their children. It's not that mom and dad don't have the right intentions at heart, but oftentimes protecting their kids feels safer and more productive than honoring and fostering them as separate beings.

That instinctual tendency in parents inhibits growth in the child because at the core of individuation is self-awareness and emotional intelligence (EQ). Defined as the capacity for introspection and the ability to recognize oneself as an individual, self-awareness encompasses understanding your personality, strengths, weaknesses, beliefs, motivations, and emotions. EQ, which differs slightly from self-awareness, refers to how someone processes and uses their emotions—both by managing them internally, and in how they respond to others.

In recent years, researchers and psychologists have been paying close attention to how these three concepts—individuation, self-awareness, and EQ—factor into how we interact with the world around us.

Emotional intelligence was first introduced as a concept in 1985, though it didn't gain momentum until the mid-90s when David Goleman published the book *Emotional Intelligence: Why It Can Matter More Than IQ*.

Since then, social scientists have been hard at work studying EQ, and Yale researchers David Caruso and Peter Salovey have advocated for the teaching of emotional intelligence in schools as a way to develop resiliency, confidence, optimism, and creativity in students.

Unfortunately, the majority of schools in America are low on the resources it takes to institute widespread changes in curricula, and the message is falling on deaf ears at home. While no one wants their child to feel overwhelmed, stressed out, or lost, parents are parenting in an era when the pressure for children to succeed is at an all-time high.

"I think parents today are in some ways reacting to the increase in competition to get into college," says Linda Morgan, author of *Beyond Smart: Boosting Your Child's Social, Emotional, and Academic Potential.* "They're reacting to the fact that the economy has had its ups and downs. They worry about their kids making it. There's more information available to everyone all the time, so it seems like things are more difficult, competitive, and stressful. It certainly raises the bar."

It would be silly to say that this competition is all in your head. The pressures your family faces are very real. But where parents of the '60s and '70s took a hands-off approach to child rearing, today's parents have overcorrected, channeling a new era of parent-as-friend, and earning themselves the moniker "helicopter parents"—hovering like drones, and monitoring their children's every move.

Morgan says she refers to these parents as "broomstick parents" because they go ahead of their kids, trying to sweep the path clear of all obstacles.

Though it may seem benign to call the coach when Jack doesn't get playing time on the basketball team, or to ring up the teacher if Jill isn't in the "right" class, Morgan says that this kind of behavior is the basis for much larger issues down the line: "In kindergarten, these kids enter school and they're smarter and more well-prepared, but they can't function by themselves on a playdate or a sleepover, even though they know how to operate an iPhone. So basically we have to start asking ourselves: are we fostering dependency? Are we raising independent and resilient kids?"

Fast forward to adolescence, and the problems only multiply. From over-parenting, a child's sense of confidence and independence is undermined, creating a culture of indecisiveness in students who aren't prepared to take the next step on their own. Even worse, because these kids have never had a chance to falter, they're rattled by minute setbacks and are increasingly unwilling to take risks.

"Kids start to think: 'I can't do this, or I can't do that' because they've learned to play it safe—because playing it safe gets them what they want," says Morgan. "They're also taking longer to grow up, which is why the 20's are now commonly considered the second adolescence."

This idea of a second adolescence, or what researcher Jeffrey Arnett calls "emerging adulthood," has become a hot topic in recent years. Arnett classifies emerging adulthood as the period between 18 and 29 years of age, as more and more young people are postponing traditional "adult" activities like getting married, buying a home, and having kids.

Arnett's research into this period of instability and uncertainty illustrates just how much the times have changed. For example, for nearly half of emerging adults, at least one of their physical moves during this time period will be back home to live with their parents. But he also says this is a time when parents and their emerging adult children can establish a new sense of "mutual respect." They should begin to relate to one another as adults, friends, and (at least near) equals.

As you read this book, ask yourself if you're hampering or supporting your child's growth as they enter emerging adulthood. To help you analyze, here's what Arnett lists as signs of growing maturity:

- *Does your child accept responsibility for him- or herself?*
- *Is your child able to make independent decisions?*
- *Is your child on the path to financial independence?*

These three criteria evolve gradually, and while no one is expecting your graduating high schooler to hit the marks on adulthood, the steps for getting your child to full independence should be clear.

THE MESSAGE WE SEND

The reason so many young adults find themselves in a "second adolescence" could, in part, be due to how our society has dismissed youth. Too often, we underestimate teenagers, minimize their feelings, and downplay their ability to hold a seat at important discussions about our communities. Students—at home, in society, and in the classroom—regularly have their opinions brushed aside. They're told to shut up and sit down in nearly every facet of their lives.

What message is this sending to our kids? *You're not good enough. You're not smart enough. Your*

*ideas and creativity don't deserve to be heard. You
don't know what's best for yourself.*

The media also plays a powerful role in disseminating this dangerous message. To see what I mean, one
only has to open the newspaper or flip on the evening
news to see stories of "out-of-control youth" who need
corralling. City councils shut down healthy outlets
like skate parks, school districts shutter programs for
art and expression, and we can forget adults asking
minors to join them at the table in important national
discussions.

When we underestimate youth and fail to invite them
to the conversation, it's a slippery slope with detrimental consequences for our communities. "What you're
implicitly teaching youth is that their voice doesn't
matter," says Daniel Gray-Kontar, a TEDx speaker and
creative arts teacher at the Cleveland School for the
Arts. "You're giving them the perspective that they
don't matter in any way, that they should not be part of
the democratic or decision-making process. Over time,
that becomes embedded in a person's personality."

This is especially problematic at school, because developing and learning to use your voice is the whole point
of education. When we don't teach kids how to use

their voice, we're setting them up for a rude awakening as soon as they step out of the protective backyard bubble. As eighteen-year-olds, they leave high school thinking their voices don't matter. But then, almost immediately, they're met with a society that's expecting them to know how to use their voice flawlessly in every circumstance.

"That's not how life works. You have to be taught how to use your voice. And increasingly, when parents—in particular parents who live in the central core, or in the inner city—when those parents are not taught how to use their voice, how in the heck are they going to teach their children how to do the same?" says Gray-Kontar.

The reverse of shutting students down, Gray-Kontar says, is empowerment. "Oftentimes, we have a really difficult time learning from the young people whom we are supposed to be raising and developing into adults. The thing about that is young people understand society in a very different way than we do. And it's very, very valid."

When we don't ask youth to be a part of the process of transforming our society, we're missing out on this whole array of potentiality that can help us in the present. "What we often say is children are the future. We have to stop saying that," Gray-Kontar says. "What we have to understand is that children are the present *as much as* they are the future."

This process of listening and learning from your child is integral to the decisions that he or she will make over the next few years. To help in this regard, I will provide you with two lists of questions at the end of each chapter. The first will be to help you evaluate the current state of your child's independence and to identify any buried biases you may have. The second list will feature conversation starters that will help you to invite your child to the discussion.

ASK YOURSELF:

- Do I feel a competitive need to get my son or daughter into a prestigious college?

- Have I, at times, talked down to youth, or minimized the validity of my child's opinions?

- What is my gut reaction about the gap year? Can I articulate why I feel the way I do?

ASK YOUR CHILD:

- Are you nervous about finishing high school?

- How do you think school is different for you than it was for me?

- Do you feel like I truly listen to you when you talk to me?

2 : GOOF-OFF YEAR

OR LIFE LAUNCH?

"In a global marketplace, it's not SAT scores and the most brilliant kid in the class who's going to get ahead. It's the one who's socially intelligent, who has a broad perspective, excellent critical thinking skills, and a high level of self-awareness."

– Drew Edwards, Executive Director, Carpe Diem Education

For many parents, the transition to college signifies an achievement eighteen years in the making. Historically, it has marked the end of childhood—the proverbial checkered flag waving a student across the finish line and on to the next phase of life. So, when a teenager decides to postpone university in favor of a gap year, it can be a tough pill for parents to swallow.

Before we move on, let's get this stat out in the open right away: nine out of ten students attend college within six months of completing a gap year, according to data from the AGA. I can almost hear what you're saying: "That's a reassuring statistic, but how can I be sure about *my* kid?"

I can't tell you whether your child will decide college is the right move after a gap year. What I can tell you is that when a gap year is done correctly, it can arm your kid with core competencies that could take years to learn in an academic setting—if they are learned at all.

Using studies of U.K. and U.S. gappers, Karl Haigler and Rae Nelson, authors of *The Gap-Year Advantage: Helping Your Child Benefit from Time Off Before or During College*, attempted to identify exactly what students gained during their time off. By examining the stories and data, they found three specific competencies kept rising to the top of the list:

- *Supporting and cooperating*
- *Leading and deciding*
- *Adapting and coping*

Show this list to any parent, and I guarantee they'll be chomping at the bit to learn how their child could excel in these traits. Haigler and Nelson break down these skills further:

- *Supporting and cooperating includes relating meaningfully to people of different backgrounds, communicating rather than suppressing feelings, and exhibiting a better sense of self.*

- *Leading and deciding deals with handling problems without the need for guidance, working well alone, and taking calculated risks based on adequate information.*

- *Adapting and coping means quickly bouncing back from setbacks and difficulties, maintaining an optimistic outlook, having confidence in uncertainty, adjusting one's personal style to suit situations and other people's characteristics, and using humor in communication.*

Scott Leroy, Associate Director of Princeton's Bridge Year Program, says he's seen firsthand how a properly structured gap year can foster these skills in students. "These are all skills that correlate highly to being successful in college, but they're also skills that not every eighteen-year-old has, at least not in any large amount. You could describe them as skills that help students be more adaptable and more resilient."

This concept of resiliency is something that Princeton's academic support office believes is an important indicator of success on campus. "It's not GPA or how good your high school was, or any of those metrics," says Leroy. "The key to being successful at Princeton is resiliency in these core competencies that allow students to adapt to a new and challenging environment."

THE CASE AGAINST THE GAP YEAR

Let's take a look at the arguments that could be made against students taking a gap year. In fairness, every parent should be aware of these, give them some thought, and consider both sides of the question.

Vern Granger is Director of Admissions and First-Year Experience at The Ohio State University. With nearly forty-five thousand undergraduates enrolled, OSU is the country's third largest public university, trumped only by Liberty University and Texas A&M. Though OSU does not publically voice support for the gap year, Granger says he recognizes that structured time off can be a positive experience for a student. He also acknowledges that some students may find it harder to get back into a school-based routine after time off.

"It's an individual experience for each student, though," he adds. "If the student has maturity, then they should be able to overcome that. Depending on the student, it could end up not being an issue whatsoever."

Stefanie DeLuca is a Johns Hopkins University researcher who studies return to college among students who take time off after high school. In her latest study, she found that students who postpone university by a year or more are 64% less likely to graduate than students who go straight through.

That's a pretty scary statistic, but before you close this book and declare the gap year a sham, let's examine the data. When we look closely, we see that DeLuca's study does not measure gap year students in particular but rather, groups them with all other students who don't immediately enter college right after high school. There are many reasons why other teens don't go to college right away: families not having enough income to cover tuition, teens getting married or having babies, and so on. It's a mistake to assume that gap year teens, known for intentional and purposeful action during their time off from formal education experience the same issues that keep other kids from immediately entering college—or graduating. In other words, to assume that gappers are less likely to graduate college than other students—on account of this broad, generalized statistic—is an unjustified conclusion.

Contrast DeLuca's study with information from other researchers, who report an increase in academic motivation in students who take a gap year. "We know that students who get to college after the gap year often have higher GPAs and academic performance. They end up being stronger students," says Joe O'Shea, Director of Undergraduate Research and Academic Engagement at Florida State University. "It is true that in some disciplines like math, if you don't use it, you lose it, and you get rusty. Students who are math majors admitted they were rusty when they came back to school, but they were much stronger as a result of their gap year experience. They had a broader lens on their education, and a broader context around mathematics as a result."

Because so many students in the U.S. take independent gap years—some estimates say as many as 70% of gappers are independent of a program—it's difficult to identify how many teens are opting to take time off. But one thing is certain: interest is definitely growing. Both anecdotal reports from college administrators and data from the USA Gap Year Fairs (the gap equivalent of college fairs) show strong increases in interest among students. Since 2010, attendance at gap year fairs has nearly tripled.

Granger says his department at OSU has seen an uptick in the number of students requesting to defer their admissions in favor of taking a gap year.

In fact, so many students have started to request deferrals that Granger's team has had to implement a formal process for evaluating deferrals in place. 2015 was the first year that they're actively tracking how many students apply to defer admissions.

"As the strength, quality, and experience of our entering class has increased, it's only natural that this is going to be a population that's really primed for wanting those additional enrichment experiences," he says.

"Universities like OSU are seeing increases in students looking for a gap year because those are the types of students looking for those growth opportunities, and being able to focus on those growth opportunities for a year without having to be enrolled in a class is what those students are looking for."

Another concern that may be raised about the gap year is the cost, an especially evident problem for lower-income families. In this case, it's not only the gap year that's the problem, but also programs like study abroad, research experiences, and internships.

"You see systemic inequality throughout higher education," says O'Shea. "The majority of students who take a gap year are going to be middle-class or above, and we need to think seriously about what kind of resources we provide for lower-income families, first-generation families, and families who have never traveled before for whom a gap year seems totally foreign, unattractive, and misguided at best." For those families, he says that getting to college is the goal and this kind of delay in matriculation seems like a total aberration from what is expected.

Jamal Grimes came from a low-income Southern community, and though he didn't do a gap year, in 2010 he was given the opportunity to test-drive an international pilot program called Global Scholars at Florida State.

Now in its fifth year, the program helps students to secure internships at non-profit organizations in developing countries across the world. Jamal traveled to Ghana, and says as the first person in his community to go international, the experience encouraged him to think more broadly about his identity:

"I come from an inner city, impoverished African-American community, so when I went to Ghana and came back, it provided more context for figuring out what it means to be African-American, and what it means to be black. I was having that debate with others because after going there, I was like, 'We are not them. We are not the same people.'"

Though Global Scholars is only a two-month program, Jamal's experience closely mirrors that of gap year students. He says that when he returned he had a renewed vigor for earning his degree in social work, and that doors opened for him that may have remained closed had he not had the chance to travel abroad. "I've always been a very reserved, introverted person, but because it was a pilot experience, I had to come back and give presentations to alumni and talk to people about it. It really opened me up to more involvement and put me in front of important people. I had more confidence in presenting to others, sharing my feelings, and talking about academics."

Still, the lack of diversity on his volunteer assignment was noticeable. "I was one of three males. It was mainly women from the U.S., Canada, and the U.K.," he says. "The community there saw women all the time, but it was very rare that men would come and volunteer. Not only that, but an African-American male was even rarer."

Today, Jamal is twenty-five-years-old and works with Florida State freshman as an academic life coach. He says he highly encourages the gap year—both as a way for students to find themselves and as a safeguard to finishing their degrees. "The reason I say that is because you have students across the country going to school, and if college was this 'end goal' for mom and dad, there are all these kids who have zero desire to be here. I have students come into my office every day, and they're stressed out, and they're pressured because their parents picked all their classes at orientation. I feel like the gap year really gives students an opportunity to go out into the world and figure out what they want to do."

SKILL ACQUISITION IN ACTION

Carlton Rounds is an academic administration veteran and current Director of Campus Engagement at Cross-Cultural Solutions, a non-profit organization that connects volunteers with people in need around the world. He says the benefits that researchers have identified as a result of the gap year come from stepping outside of your comfort zone, making mistakes, and learning from people around you. At CCS, gappers volunteer alongside individuals of varying ages who come from different backgrounds—a rich opportunity for young people who haven't yet ventured outside their peer circles.

He tells the story of a time when he was thirty-nine-years-old and shared an experience with an eighteen-year-old who was volunteering at a special education center: "At dinner, we would talk about our volunteer work days, and this younger guy was a street artist, so he loved to just sit and sketch. Then one day he said, 'I don't know what to do about this issue that's happening on-site at my placement.' I said, 'Okay, we'll make a deal. I'll teach you some special education techniques if you'll give your personal time to bring art to people on my placement.' I could never have replicated his skills, as I have no artistic talent. One of the big, important outcomes for him was that he asked for help from an adult in exchange for his own mature talents. I think that's a huge lesson in reciprocity."

Experiences like this one translate to increased self-confidence in everyday life. When a student forms a relationship with an adult who isn't in their family, it helps their interactions in college and beyond. "Maybe your child will be afraid to talk to his professors when he goes to school, but now he's not afraid anymore because he has an independently established friend who's older than he is. One success with one adult leads to better communication skills with teachers and advisors at school or work," says Rounds.

Sophie Abo first heard about the gap year through a friend's sister. Sophie's family has always valued travel, so when she brought up the concept of taking a year off to explore, her parents were onboard. For the first part of the year, Sophie traveled through Asia with a program, and then set off on her own with a friend to traverse India and Nepal. Of her experience she says: "I feel much more like a real person now. I've lived on my own for the year, and I'm no longer that eighteen-year-old living at home with my parents. I'm motivated to keep up with the world, and I'm more aware of different cultures and global politics."

Donna Morgan saw her own daughter return from a gap year more confident in her choices, more mature, and totally comfortable in her own skin. "She was at college orientation, and other kids were asking their parents, 'Do you think I should take this? What should I do?' Betsy had it all figured out, and she's just raring to go."

CURBING BURN-OUT AND
FOSTERING DISCOVERY

Something else to think about when considering time off is your child's trajectory to this point. Most likely, they hopped on the school treadmill at the age of five and have been running full-tilt ever since. Very few students —even, and possibly especially, if they're high achievers—benefit from this intense pounding of information. Among educators, there's a joke that says if Rip Van Winkle awoke today, he'd recognize nothing, except for a high school classroom. The sad truth is that very little has changed in America's schooling system in the last two centuries.

In talking about how we learn, memory trainer Jim Kwik says that the challenge we need to overcome is that we grew up with a 20th century education. "A 20th century education was an assembly line, a one-size-fits-all, cookie-cutter approach to learning. It was about pushing information into someone's head: sit quietly by yourself and don't talk to your neighbor. But that's not the world we live in anymore. The age that we live in right now is the age of electric cars and space ships that are going to Mars, but our vehicle of choice in transportation is the horse and buggy."

When we should be redefining and restructuring our education system, instead we're encouraging teachers to continue to teach in this passive way. "20th century education trained us to be passive," says Kwik. "A teacher is pushing information inside your mind, and you're just consuming it. You can't learn like that today because in today's information age, that's like taking a sip of water from a fire hose."

Rather than reward teachers who innovate in this new age, we're instead evaluating their performance based on students' ability to pass a state-issued test. This encourages teachers to value rote memorization and standardization over creativity and customization. There's a huge divide in how we're teaching and how students are learning. See the problem?

It's not all bad news. While it's true that students might dislike school, we shouldn't assume they dislike learning. In most cases, quite the opposite is true. "Students want to feel a connection to what they're studying. They want to be attached to their learning," says Sarah Persha, an independent education counselor, psychologist, and director of education at the American Gap Association. "I very much believe that young people love to learn if they're learning in a way that works for them. Many of them need a combination of formats for their learning: experiential learning, learning abroad, pushing one's comfort zones. These are all things I've seen students really benefit from."

When we frame the discussion about how students learn this way, we realize that the traditional model is one-sided and linear. Very little room is left for exploratory exposure, which we know, without a shadow of a doubt, is instrumental in developing creative, curious learners.

THE EFFECT OF EXPOSURE TO EXPERIENCES ON CAREER CHOICE

"There's a whole body of research in career development on 'chance encounters' where people end up going down a career path based on a random meeting they had on a train, or someone they talked to who did something interesting. Exposure is important," says psychologist Karen Bridbord.

If all the research indicates that a year of exposure and exploration doesn't hinder the progression of a gap year student's eventual decision to attend university, then I think it's time we ask ourselves: what's the big rush? Author Linda Morgan says often the rush is driven by parents who are hyper-worried and hyper-vigilant because they're hearing about a select group of very successful kids, or about kids who can't get into college. "The reality is your child can get into college, and there's a college for everybody, but the conversation is all about the top twenty that are very competitive and hard to get into. You see the words 'Ivy League' in every article about schools, which is just ridiculous. We're talking about a subset, but parents don't really see that."

In fact, even the Ivys promote time off before or during college as a way to get the full benefit of formalized education. An article titled "Time Out or Burn Out for the Next Generation"—co-written by Harvard's dean of admissions, director of admissions, and an adjunct lecturer in psychology—makes the case for postponing entrance to college for a year. It even credits Harvard's graduation rate—one of the highest in the nation—"perhaps in part because so many students take time off."

The article also states: "Parents worry that their sons and daughters will be sidetracked from college and may never enroll. [They] fear that taking time off can cause students to 'fall behind' or lose their study skills irrevocably. That fear is rarely justified."

Sophie Abo says she's more inclined to favor a less traditional path after her gap year experience: "I would encourage students who are on a very linear journey taking one class right after another to get out and experiment a bit more—really learning about everything that's out there, and then choosing something, instead of streamlining their education."

THE ANTI-COLLEGE PERSPECTIVE

There's a growing body of opposition to our linear education model. James Altucher, author of *Choose Yourself: Be Happy, Make Millions, Live the Dream*, argues altogether against sending your kids to college. He says that students today would be better served to do just about anything else that includes hands-on learning. When asked about the assumption that people who go to college make more money than their peers who don't, here's the response he posted to his blog:

"First off: the study is completely fake, and anyone who took Statistics 101 in college knows that, but I'll get to that in a second. Think about twenty years ago. College was cheaper. There weren't as many reasons not to go. And there weren't as many alternatives as there are now. So what did smart, ambitious kids do? They went to college. What did kids who did not feel as ambitious do? They didn't go to college. So the study has what is called 'Selection Bias.' They assumed they

had one audience in their group that they were testing (people who went to college) but, in fact, they really had a completely different group (smart, ambitious kids versus not-as-ambitious kids).

"A true test would be to take two-thousand kids accepted by a wide variety of colleges. Then say to half the kids, "You can never go to college." And then in twenty years see who made more income. My guess is the group that did not go to college. How come? Because they would have a five-year head start. They would not be required to study a bunch of classes they didn't want to take in the first place and would never remember, and they would have the enormous gift of not having to be perhaps hundreds of thousands of dollars in debt. Or even tens of thousands of dollars in debt, which is still too much for a twenty-three-year-old."

Uncollege, a program that encourages students to forgo university in favor of real-world experience, is also gaining momentum. Their mission is to help students gain the skills necessary to succeed in today's world through mentorship, one-on-one coaching, entrepreneurship, and practice, in lieu of a traditional degree program. At $16,000, the one-year program is significantly cheaper than any four-year school.

Despite the advances in the anti-college movement, these opinions represent a small minority. Surprisingly, even 75% of Uncollege's student population go on to school after their time in the program. When I asked Dale Stephens, Uncollege's founder, about his organization's stance on post-secondary, he said it really depends on what the student wants to do: "We have people who want to become environmental scientists, engineers, and doctors, and so then we work with them to figure out the right path to get them into college. The people who want to become singer-songwriters? College might not make sense, so we work with them to gain the right skills, build the right relationships, and have enough footing at the end of the year to go off and pursue that."

Regardless of the programs and opinions popping up, the vast majority of parents and students still look to college as a rite of passage, though perhaps increasingly, as a means to an end.

THE COLLEGE PERSPECTIVE

You'd be hard-pressed to find a college admissions counselor or even an employer who would turn up their nose at applicants who have spent time reflecting and learning about what makes them tick. And while not all colleges are onboard quite yet, more and more are realizing that taking a year off for reflection can be a powerful way to enter the next stage of the journey with more clarity and a stronger sense of direction.

As recently as two years ago, O'Shea says that Florida State was saying no to gap years, and to students who wanted to defer. But now they've instituted a formalized, transparent process that allows applying students to take a gap year. The school's change of heart centers on two key drivers:

First, FSU has come to believe that allowing students to take a gap year will improve the school's retention and graduation rates. "We think gap years are an important tool in our toolbox to help students succeed in higher education—just like advisors, tutors, coaches, and the other kinds of interventions we have to support students," O'Shea explains. "A gap year crystallizes students' life plans, helps them mature, and gives them a sense of purpose and groundedness that enables them to do really well in college and ultimately, to get more out of it."

Second, the school has come to see the gap year as a vehicle to attract strong students to the university. So much so that FSU is unrolling a new policy to give away

$50,000 to gappers (up to $5,000 for each student). To be considered, students who apply to take the deferral must write an essay outlining their educational goals and how they think a gap year will enrich their future trajectory.

"We're serious about democratizing access," says O'Shea. "And we think the policy will help us attract top students to the university. It's a longer investment strategy with a heavy front-end investment for us, but we think it will pay off."

He adds that this shift in opinion at the collegiate level is a trend that will only continue to snowball. "Colleges are increasingly accepting gap year deferments and setting up special processes. There's still a long way to go to change the culture on this, but it will happen."

This trend is being driven by the students—as the college landscape gets more competitive, schools will have no choice but to become more accommodating. At the same time, schools are starting to understand that the gap year facilitates important changes in the lives of young adults coming onto campus. For this reason, schools are increasingly willing to cooperate with student applicants wanting deferrals.

Carlton Rounds thinks of the gap year as an opportunity for students to process their childhood in a way that allows them to decide what kind of adult they want to be. In order to do that, though, it's imperative the person be in a new environment—ideally in surroundings that act as a catalyst for confidence and identity building. At the end of the day, you can't put the same old stuff in and expect something new to come out.

Unfortunately, the freshman year in college is just about the worst place to try to develop this skill. For one thing, it's the first time many teens have been unsupervised, so they're likely to waste their first year hungover and uninterested in entry-level coursework. I know in my circle of friends and acquaintances, very few even remember the majority of freshman year—and most would probably tell you they certainly didn't learn anything academically enriching. "For many people, the first year of college is wasted," says Tuft's Mindy Nierenberg. "But I've met a lot of gap year students, and they all say the same thing: instead of being burned out academically, they are so excited to get back to academics. They have more motivation and more direction."

She also says that because gappers have had to deal with pretty big issues—like speaking a new language, understanding a different culture, or living with a homestay family, they're better prepared to handle the transition to college. "They've dealt with some really difficult things, so having freedom on campus doesn't seem like as big a deal."

For parents concerned that their teen will fly off the rails at their first taste of freedom during a gap year, Jason Sarouhan has some advice: "Students and parents need to align with mentors that they trust. So even if a student is taking a more self-directed path, I would really want to be sure that there is an adult around who has the best interests of safety and overall experience in mind."

WHY COLLEGE NEEDS HELP

Previously, colleges were the answer to escaping menial work or grueling physical labor. They were, above all, a promise—go to college and you'll land a good job that keeps food on the table, allows your family to go on vacations, and doesn't keep you chained to the factory line or breaking your back on the farm.

Today, that "sure bet" is an increasingly risky move. More kids go to college today than ever before, so there's way more competition for "the good jobs" than when earlier generations of college grads entered the market. Probably everyone knows at least one degreed young person who's still living with their parents, depressed and working a tedious job, or not working at all. When we consider that average salaries among young college grads decreased by 8.5% between 2000 and 2012, the picture gets even grimmer.

Students nowadays are exhausted from the hamster wheel of piano lessons, basketball practice, Mandarin class, and the marathon effort it takes to ace the next test. More than ever, teachers are teaching not to a student's sense of self and curiosity, but instead to a set of government-issued tests that determines who succeeds and who gets left behind. When you stop to take a hard look at the race for the collegiate top, it's not hard to see why students are more depressed and anxious today than in generations past.

"High school students are on an academic treadmill, and they're gearing themselves toward admission to college," says Nierenberg. "In order to get into a school like Tufts, they need so many different accomplishments. Even their extracurriculars are purposeful, so they're not really taking risks or thinking outside the box. They're also not really taking the time to think about the meaning of their life."

Many parents think if their child steps off the tread-mill—even temporarily— they'll be disqualified from the chance to reap the benefits of their hard work. Nierenberg says that's simply not the case. "During a gap year, students are able to put themselves outside of their regular circle of experience. This allows them to be challenged by working with others in a culture that's different than their own, or gives them the chance to try out different passions that they may have thought about but haven't explored."

SURVEYING THE GAP YEAR BENEFITS

I'm highly skeptical about nearly everything, so when I started researching gap years, I dove headfirst into the data rather than the anecdotal. What I uncovered was pretty astonishing.

The American Gap Association shows that students who take a gap year before college head to school more focused: they switch majors less, study more, finish in less time than their non-gap year peers, and report higher GPAs.

"Something I hear often from parents is that it took them so much effort to get their child through high school," says Rounds. "They'll say something like, 'We had a tutor because Johnny wasn't so good at math, maybe his executive functions were weak and we had to give some support for that, but he's done so well, and we're so proud of him. But if we let him off of his regimented trajectory, his academic skills will atrophy, so when he goes in as a college freshman, he won't do well.'"

If this sounds familiar to you, take a moment to ponder your real concern. Let's say you're worried that your child's academics will suffer. What do you really mean? Are you worried about focus? Retention? Or is it something more specific, such as your child may forget all of his geometry?

"A good gap year program will actually improve academic and intellectual acuity because focus is related to self-confidence and a sense of increasing challenge over time," says Rounds. "And in the context of service [volunteer work], you're not being graded, you're being worse than graded; you are facing direct social consequences. In this case, if the student doesn't perform the task, then fourteen kids aren't going to eat lunch."

INSURANCE FOR COLLEGE

Unfortunately, in the U.S., there's a stigma associated with taking a break from the formal education system. Even in the most confident students and parents, fears about getting left behind, or being viewed as "less than," are enough to crush the conversation before it ever gets going. But there's evidence to support that a gap year isn't just a chance to relax—it's a chance to ensure your investment in higher education.

Consider this common story of a college freshman: Brendan goes into class burnt-out, disengaged, or uninterested in academics. Unsurprisingly, he doesn't do well and ends up with a C–average, though he realizes through the process who he really is and what he really wants. Once he has a little clarity on the situation, he thinks, "This is not the right school for me. It's too competitive, it's not friendly, and it doesn't have a community I like or feel supported in." But then, it's not easy for him to transfer if he has a record of not doing well.

"Families are going to spend a quarter of a million dollars on this education. How about $20,000 to launch this person's life in a way that most other developed societies have already discovered creates remarkable citizens who have a greater sense of happiness and well-being?" asks Rounds.

My alma mater, Ohio University, doesn't have a gap year program, but when I reached out to Patti McSteen,

Associate Dean of Students at OU, she made the case for buffering the investment in college with a gap year: "To send a traditionally-aged college student to university when they are not emotionally or academically ready is an enormous financial risk. Where else would you make a $60,000 to $100,000 commitment to something without feeling confident of why you are doing this, or without a clear sense of readiness?"

She continues: "When you look at the amount of money some families invest in 'elite' youth sports camps and trainings, it's absurd to me that they don't put the same amount of planning and 'training' into their child's success as a college student. Taking a gap year to prepare for success is one way of doing that."

Drew Edwards, Executive Director of Carpe Diem Education (a gap year program focused on community, cultural immersion, service learning, and adventure) seconds McSteen's opinion. "College is one of the biggest investments you're ever going to make for your child. For me, it's the difference of a kid going to college because they want to, as opposed to simply because they *should*."

That distinction between desire and obligation is crucial. Students who want to go—who have possibly traveled the world for a year, working in remote places, challenging themselves, and encountering poverty—are going to relate very differently to the college experience. They're going to know themselves so much more, and therefore fit into situations they encounter in ways that feel more authentic. When you look at what happens in a gap year—the social and emotional growth, the global perspective, the interpersonal skill development, in addition to the positive data surrounding performance at school—you're in every possible way setting your child up to take advantage of the biggest investment you're ever going to make on their behalf.

Another parent I spoke to frames the situation a little differently: "As a parent, it's important to be realistic about your kid. After a good gap year, they're going to understand a lot better what a college education gets them rather than going in three months after high school. If they were on a college track before, they're pretty unlikely to not see the benefit of what college can do for them after the gap. And if a gap year gets them off college, it will get them onto something that they're really passionate about in life. That's not a bad thing."

Betsy Morgan, who traveled through South America with Carpe Diem, says her gap year made her feel so much more confident in her decision to go to school, and gave her clarity on what she wanted to study:

"I'm in a better position to take advantage of school than had I gone straight through. College is an investment, so spending the freshman year bumming around and not knowing anything, or partying a lot, is not the best use of time. Looking back, I wish I could tell myself, 'A gap year will make you so much more prepared for college, and so much readier to get more out of college.' It's so funny to compare the differences between prepping for college last summer and this summer. I still feel that nervous excitement, but there's none of the crushing anxiety of, 'Did I make the right choice?'"

Gap year programs aren't trying to replace college. If anything, they're a preparation for it. "We are not trying to stand apart from higher education, we are *a part* of higher education," says Drew Edwards.

ASK YOURSELF:

- What are your main concerns about your child not going to college right away?

- What skills do you want your child to have as an adult?

- In what ways have you enabled your child to make his or her own decisions?

- Does your child have a strong leaning to major in a particular subject? Is this inclination driven by something more than an obligation to choose?

- What would happen if your child chose not to go to college?

- Is your child prepared to take college seriously?

- What's the rush?

ASK YOUR CHILD:

Instead of approaching your student about college or the gap year with your own ideas of what should happen, frame the discussion as though you're working to plan the next stage together. Your son or daughter is no longer a child, and this is a prime opportunity to empower him or her to start taking control of life.

Start with questions like these:

- If you could plan the best year ever, what would it look like?

- Do you want to travel?

- How do you feel about working for a while before college?

- Do you feel burnt out on school?

- What would happen if you took a break from school?

- Do you want to go to school right now? Why or why not?

- What are you expecting to happen in the next year?

- If you couldn't go to school, what would you do? How would you feel?

3: DORITOS, VIDEOGAMES, AND THE DREADED COUCH POTATO

"Students have told me that they don't think college is right for them at this particular moment, but they don't know what they would do if they weren't here. Oftentimes, it is a maturity thing, but sometimes it's just the effects of an over-scheduled childhood, followed by an overly stressful high school. Students have never had time to just be."

– Patti McSteen, Associate Dean of Students, Ohio University

For students who have never spent time away from the home, the question of maturity level often comes up alongside the discussion of the gap year. A parent may ask: what if my child isn't mature enough to excel in a different environment?

"There's a difference between immaturity, naivety, and youth," says Carlton Rounds. "Immaturity is not governed by only one age group. Immaturity can be a lifelong struggle. But when we're dealing with gap programs, it's important to set up a dynamic of respect from the start."

What Rounds is promoting is the notion that when kids are treated with respect, given an opportunity to do real tasks, and then asked to reflect on their experiences, they usually outperform the expectations many adults have for them. So, the issue of immaturity we're talking about? In some respects, it's rarely an issue at all.

That doesn't mean that students set out on a gap year and automatically transform into self-aware adults. Rounds says that throughout his years working with young people in education, he's seen everything from gender, race, region, and class affect how long it takes for a child to move through adolescence into the next stage of emerging adulthood. He also says that some-times it's hard to know, when you're looking at a young person, how to gauge the speed at which they'll develop.

"I sometimes think I wish I could just find the exact perfect combo to help them 'get it,' and the only thing I've ever seen in my entire life that can have that effect is international experience and service," he says. "Having to be responsible and having to answer to someone else who's different than you, and in a situation where you're held accountable, is transformative. And this isn't an accountability that's meant to shame you if you don't step up. It's a deeper experience than that. I think teenagers in particular are ravenously hungry for deep, authentic, and independent experiences."

NEW IDENTITY

For many students, a gap year can open their eyes to the world outside of their community—it's no longer playtime, and when students realize that, they rise to the occasion accordingly. It's also a critical time for identity formation and character development.

Most students don't really know what their identity is until they have life experiences under their belts, and figuring out who they are away from everyone they know can lead to positive learning.

Perhaps the quiet and more introverted teen finds out that she is well-liked, respected, and good at what she does. How great is that? Or, maybe for another, he discovers he has to work harder and give more of himself to be both socially rewarded by his peers and to be a better volunteer. "It's a lot nicer to address this kind of feedback away from everyone you know, so that you have freedom from past perceptions and opinions," says Rounds. "For some, it can be an opportunity to reinvent themselves."

When we look at what's going on developmentally in this age group, the concept of peer and group feedback makes perfect sense. At this age, students are much more open to peer learning than to having an adult tell them what to do. Any parent of a teen has probably realized this lesson over and over...and over again, throughout the high school years.

When students are in small groups designed to give peer feedback, an environment is created that allows the group to work out any immaturity in a healthy manner. They're not isolated or being made fun of, but are being held accountable by their peers in a new way.

"When that immaturity manifests in, say, showing up late for a volunteer project, or sleeping in, or making inappropriate comments, ideally we're at a place where we can confront that openly. We have the students talk about it, share how it makes them feel, or the impact it has on them, and it creates this peer network of support," Edwards says.

Obviously, this idyllic scenario doesn't always take flight with zero snags, but as a program progresses, more collaboration and peer-directed learning can be expected. Edwards says issues surrounding maturity come up on every trip but what's remarkable is how responsive students are to the feedback of their peers. "In every way, whenever you can create a safe environment that actively offers opportunities to give and receive feedback in healthy ways, then it's no longer a threat."

Instead of the internal dialogue of "I'm bad" or "I'm wrong," it shifts the awareness to, "Oh, my actions are having an impact on this other person. Maybe I can be more mindful and aware of that."

What about bullying? Can that be a problem on a gap year? For teens who have been bullied or ostracized in high school, the idea of leaving a supportive family environment can be terrifying. Teenagers are notorious for being cruel to each other, so how can you be certain your son or daughter won't be persecuted in a gap year situation?

While there's only so much that group leaders can do to foster a culture of inclusivity, Sarouhan says at its heart, a well-structured, intentional gap year program is going to go above and beyond to build compassion and empathy, encourage tolerance and understanding of differences, and build a young adult's capacity for insightful reflection and communication.

"While I have seen many successes of more reserved students 'blossoming' and finding their voices in the program, I will also note that a gap year, in general, and a facilitated gap year program, specifically, is not necessarily a magic elixir for a student who is particularly withdrawn or has low self-confidence," he elaborates. "I have certainly observed group settings that were deeply inclusive and understanding, and yet included students who were removed or did not feel connected with their peers."

He says that sometimes these students are able to rise up to meet the welcoming embrace of the group, and other times they never find the courage or self-esteem to do so: "As with all human relationships, both parties must come together to collaborate and create something amazing."

His advice to a family with a child who has been isolated, ostracized, or bullied? Invest in an emotionally intelligent and highly reflective program. Ideally this program will have a balanced gender make-up and will incorporate activities that your teen already enjoys or feels comfortable with. "Giving your child as many opportunities as you can to make personal connections in the group will help support their feeling included, and activities within their comfort zone will boost confidence to engage in experiences that they may feel less confident about," says Sarouhan.

One thing you should steer clear of is encouraging your reserved teen to sign on for a highly independent gap experience where he or she is solely responsible for making friends and building up a support network. "Gap year has the potential to be transformative, but setting the stage for success is a key part of planning for this journey," Sarouhan adds.

If you're still unsure about whether your shy son or daughter would thrive in a gap environment, I'd recommend seeking out the advice of a gap year counselor, or in more extreme cases, a psychotherapist. Unlike myself, a trained professional will be able to evaluate your teen's individual situation and predict the likelihood of gap year success.

WORKING FOR THE BENEFIT OF ALL

In a gap year program, students may find it's the first time expectations are raised concerning them and their actions. Now, it's not only about what they want; it's about what it takes to be a functioning member of a group.

When Riley Wong returned home from his gap year in South America, his new "willingness to help the group" mentality was an unexpected—and welcome—development for his parents. By learning how to function as part of a group in his time away, Riley learned that when everyone contributes and does their job well, the group works better and everyone is happier.

"We're his group now, so he mows the lawn, he makes dinner, he texts his sister to ask if she needs help with her homework," says Riley's mom, Pia Wong. "I was in San Francisco recently on a Saturday, which is our family's laundry day, and he texted me to ask if there was anything special he needed to do with the last two loads of laundry! I was floored. I wanted to ask him what he'd done with my son. I know with certainty that my friends with kids who went straight into college are not having a similar experience."

Along with increased attentiveness, a gap year can

also instill a sense of curiosity in students that nudges them forward on the scale of maturity. For Riley, Pia says he's more open-minded and interested in world politics after his time away. "We have a subscription to *The Economist,* and he reads it with a notepad, taking notes. Now he cares more about what's going on because his international experience makes it much more real."

I spoke with another parent of a gapper who said her daughter's initial gap experience emboldened her to plan two more trips before fall semester—one to Colorado to work on a farm-to-table program, and another to a horse rescue in Florida. "She said to me, 'Mom, this is really who I am and what I want to do. I need to be on the move.' To talk to her now, she's very focused and knows what she wants. I have no concerns about her going off to college now. She's already kind of done it."

A MENTAL TUNE-UP

If you're concerned about whether your child will take a gap year seriously, or that they won't know the rules of the road when they get in-country, there are good ways to help kick their thought process into gear.

Whether they're going to Detroit or Ethiopia,

educating them on issues of diversity is a necessity. "Help them to understand and be open to perspectives that are different than their own," recommends Mindy Nierenberg. "They should really be prepared to leave their judgments behind and be very humble."

She says you can also remind them that everyone has a story to tell, and that being open to sharing their story can be a gift to others. Conversely, when people share their story, talk to your child about how that's a gift someone is giving to them.

ASK YOURSELF:

- In what ways do I hold my child accountable?

- Do I invite my child to be more mature in everyday interactions? How?

- What kind of adult do I want my child to be? Am I encouraging that development with my actions?

- Can my child describe his/her own personality characteristics?

- How would my child benefit from different interactions and experiences?

- How would I rank my child's current maturity level?

- How does my child's maturity level stack up in

comparison to his/her peers?

- What types of experiences would help my child grow his/her awareness?

ASK YOUR CHILD:

- What excites you most about meeting people who are different from you?

- What strengths and experiences can you share with others?

- Why is it something special when another person shares a personal story about themselves with you?

- What are you expecting the experience of college or a gap year will be like?

- How do you think you would like living away from home and working with a group of people your own age?

- Do you think homesickness will be an issue when you leave home?

4: LOST IN THE

OCEAN OF CHOICE

"The difference between a richly positive experience and a mediocre one might be how involved the young adult has been in discovering what suits him or her."

– Diane Geller, Independent Educational Consultant

Once you decide to look into what a gap year entails, you'll be thinking one thing: "Where the *&$!*# do we start?" A Google search for gap year programs returns over twenty-four million results, which means there's enough to keep you busy for years.

Holly Swartz says she felt overwhelmed when her daughter, Lucy, first started considering a gap year. "I was bewildered trying to figure out the logistics of how to organize a year because I had no models in my head of what that should look like, or where to turn, or what would constitute a reasonable use of an entire year."

Luckily, as the gap year movement has grown in the last decade, so have the resources available to you and your family. From online communities to more personalized, one-on-one experiences with higher education counselors and professionals, there's plenty of help if you know where to look.

Before we dive into how to find help, I want to take a step back. As I mentioned earlier, there are two routes to taking a gap year. The first is to join a program, and the second is for the student to plan activities on his or her own during a self-directed year. Let's talk programs first.

GAP YEAR PROGRAMS

Programs run the gamut in terms of what they offer, from service-based assignments to adventure-fueled excursions. A good way to start exploring options is by checking out the American Gap Association's accredited programs, and working your way out from there. You can also Google "gap year programs + [your teen's interests]" and see what pops up.

Websites like GoOverseas.com are also helpful. On the website, parents and students can search an online directory for all kinds of programs abroad. Broken up into different categories—study, teach, intern, and volunteer—the site is neutral territory for all program providers.

"Our goal is to be a comprehensive site, and we put a lot of value into putting every opportunity up there whether it's good or bad," says Mandi Schmitt, Director for Gap Years at GoOverseas. "The hope is that through alumni reviews, visitors can judge the validity of a program for themselves. Our policy is to never remove a review that's written by a valid participant."

If you're able, it's also a good idea to meet program representatives face-to-face at a gap year fair. Similar to college fairs, the USA Gap Year Fairs started in 2006 as a way to introduce gap years and program providers to families. The fairs have exploded since their inception, and in 2014, five thousand visitors attended thirty-five events where nearly one hundred different programs were represented.

"There's something incredible about actually going to a gap year fair, especially if you're thinking that you're the only one in your area considering a gap year," says

Kathy Cheng, Director at USA Gap Year Fairs and Director of Admissions at Dynamy. "You may feel like, 'What am I doing? Is this a good choice?' But then you show up to a fair, and there are five hundred other people, and you realize, 'Okay, there is some momentum behind this. There's a community here.'"

Because families can't travel to every country to vet programs and determine the best ones, these events are a good place to get a feel for the different types of gap years, gather intel, and meet program providers and counselors. The fairs travel the country from January through February. Visit www.usagapyearfairs.org to find out when a gap year fair is happening near you.

To further help guide you in your research, I've included a list of gap year resources on my website at www.andreawien.com/gapyears. There, you'll find updated links to aggregate websites such as GoOverseas, and the AGA's accredited programs, plus downloadable checklists, educational consultants, and more.

INDEPENDENT OR SELF-DIRECTED GAP YEARS

As for independent gap years, it's slightly harder to narrow down the options. Some students spend time hiking the Appalachian Trail, working at a neighborhood café, or volunteering at a cousin's school. If you think an independent gap year is the way to go, it's best to keep an open dialogue with your teen about their wants and desires, then try to match them with experiences they'll find enriching. Because it can be overwhelming to start, it can also help to bring in professional help in the form of an educational consultant.

An educational consultant works with your teen to identify interests and ballpark career options, and to decide whether a gap year could be the right choice. Along with Interim's services that I mentioned earlier, you can also search for an educational consultant on the Independent Educational Consultants Association website at iecaonline.com. The IECA is a not-for-profit, international organization that aims to promote educational consulting for academic and professional guidance and development. Additionally, Certified Educational Planners has a list of certified educational planners on their website at aicep.org.

Even if you find a consultant through these channels, be aware that not all consultants are created equal. Because gap years are still a relatively fledgling concept in the U.S., many educational consultants may be unknowledgeable about the details of a gap year, or the appropriate programs to look into. If you come across someone who is unwilling or unable to help you in regard to gap years, keep looking.

"I think the big thing is to make sure your consultant has put a gap year on the college list as an option, even if you eventually reject it. The role of a consultant is to help the student see options and keep the options open," says Diane Geller, co-founder of DeFelice & Geller, an educational consultancy. She also recommends asking any potential consultants these questions before hiring:

- *Tell me about your background—how long have you been an educational consultant?*

- *How do you keep up with new trends, application changes and laws?*

- *What professional associations do you belong to?*

- *Do you ever accept compensation from colleges? (The answer should be no.)*

- *Do you guarantee admission to a school or a certain minimum dollar value in scholarship? (The answer should be no.)*

- *Will you write and/or re-write essays for the student? (The answer should be no.)*

- *Will you use your personal contacts to get my child into a top college? (The answer should be no.)*

Whether you're working with a consultant or researching gap year possibilities independently, the best place to start is with your child's interests. "A gap year is best served if a student spends it as an opportunity to explore what they're already interested in," says Ethan Knight, President of the American Gap Association. "It's essentially an opportunity to see if what you love to do can turn into something you can get paid to do."

Once you've identified your child's interests—say, in African culture, or in working with small kids—you can start to tailor your search to programs or experiences that align with those interests.

When Lucy Buckman was debating how to spend her gap year, she knew language learning in South America was something she wanted to explore. "I had been studying Spanish for many years, so I knew one of the main things was that I wanted to get my Spanish more functional," Lucy explains. "I ended up living with a host family in Peru while I volunteered and studied Spanish." Because Lucy knew she wanted to live with a family in a Spanish-speaking country, she hit Google and started plugging in relevant keywords. Of course, not everything online is reputable, so I'll talk about how to qualify programs in a moment.

A program can instill confidence in students, and the security of joining a developed program versus going at it alone shouldn't be discounted. A program does offer stability and safety while still allowing your child to develop a sense of independence away from your family structure. But it's not the only way. Rob Spach's son Christopher pieced together an impressive gap year that included working at a local health food store, volunteering in Nicaragua, and joining the Iona Community in Scotland. Along with fostering a strong sense of maturity, confidence, and independence, Christopher's work at the health food store gave him a deeper sense of himself in a completely unexpected way.

"Working at the store was a great experience because it was a whole different industry for him. He was getting experience with different foods, learning about food, and thinking about food issues. Through all of this, he got really interested in veganism, and he's now a vegan," says Christopher's dad.

STAYING DOMESTIC DURING A GAP YEAR

Gap years are individual experiences and should be planned as such. What is right for one student may be completely wrong for another. This means that going international isn't right for every teen.

For example, if your son or daughter is shy or anxious, shipping them off on a fast-paced trip to India might not be the smartest move. In that case, a domestic program like the one offered by Dynamy could be a better fit. During Dynamy's Internship Year, students live in monitored apartments in Worchester, Massachusetts, and intern at a number of different businesses in the area.

"We get some students who may be a little more introverted—they may feel like jumping on a plane to go change the world is daunting," says Dynamy's Fred Kaelin. "Our students get guidance in addition to interning, volunteering, and doing a bit of adventure. That combination is interesting to them because they get to be part of a community of about fifty students and have quality one-on-one time with our advisors."

Even teens who are confident travelers may find that staying stateside is a wiser choice, depending on the goal of their time off. Dynamy's Director of Admissions, Kathy Cheng, says really narrowing down the goal of the gap year is critical in deciding whether international or domestic is right: "If the goal is language immersion, I would say to go abroad. But if a student says, 'I have no idea what I want to do with my life and I want to figure that out,' then a domestic program like Dynamy may be a good fit. Students can try out three different internships at Dynamy in three different industries, and that can really help them find some answers."

A domestic program can also help to buffer the transition from high school into the real world. "With our students, we look at things like, how do you contribute to the work force? What's apartment life like? What are the societal norms within the U.S.? How do you work and create your own space within our society?" Cheng continues. "I think there's a lot to be said about domestic gap year programs because they not only teach students what the U.S. has to offer, but also what life may actually be like after the college experience."

When Cheng mentioned this idea of teaching students what the U.S. has to offer, it struck a familiar chord with me. I remember being rocked with culture shock during a high school volunteer assignment in West Virginia. I lived only a few hours away, but before the trip I had no idea how differently people lived in the poorer neighborhoods of Appalachia. It felt a million miles away, and I'd barely traveled at all.

When I tell Cheng this, she says, "It's great to think America is the greatest country in the world, and that we're so well-developed that we have to go to these 'developing countries,' but there's so much need here that people often forget about." For students who crave to make a difference, it's powerful to remember that help may be even more needed at home than it is abroad.

If your teen is after adventure rather than service, they'll be happy to hear that it's possible to stay local and still feed their inner adrenaline junkie. At Outward Bound, another program that offers both domestic and international placements, students can go backpacking in the Rockies, sailing around Washington State's San Juan Islands, or kayaking in Florida. Outward Bound was started in 1941, and every year nearly two hundred thousand students participate in its programs.

BEST PRACTICES

Regardless of which path your child chooses to take, there are a few best practices to maximize the chances for success. For starters, establish a list for every member of the family that addresses concerns and questions. You can find a list of potential questions in the resources section of the American Gap Association website. Sarah Persha, the AGA's education director, says making their own list helps parents and students see where their concerns are different, which lays the framework for a productive discussion of expectations.

To begin, discuss the following with your child:

- *Where do you want to sleep at night? Do you want to camp, or would you like to stay in a home?*

- *Should we be able to be easily in touch with each other? If not, when are the times that we should know we can be in touch?*

- *Do you want to travel or stay in one location?*

- *How many people would you prefer to have in your group?*

- *What will be the structure and supervision?*

- *What kind of environment do you want to be in? Urban, backwoods, suburban?*

- *Do you want to include a service (volunteer) component?*

- *Do you want to live with other students, or stay with a homestay family?*

- *Is there a certain subject of interest you wish to pursue in your gap year?*

- *What do you want to accomplish in the gap year?*

You need to think through everything in terms of what your child wants and needs, so setting aside time to have these conversations can help maintain sanity in your home. At the same time, though, be careful not to overload your child with discussion, or constantly pepper him or her with questions. "If you don't set aside specific times to have these discussions, it can become all-consuming," says educational consultant Diane Geller. "Sometimes parents get so enthused with something that it overshadows the child's interest."

Remember that deciding on a gap year isn't the only thing on your child's mind. During this busy time, they could also be dealing with school, extracurriculars, exams, and friends—not to mention a rollercoaster of emotions about transitioning out of high school. "I often remind parents that it's important to remember who's having the gap experience. A gap year shouldn't just be about satisfying a parental lust for adventure," advises Geller.

It can be reassuring to realize that you don't have to plan the entire year out from the get-go. When Betsy Morgan was deciding what her gap year would look like, she met with her mom to talk about progress and options every Sunday night. As her gap year unfolded, they planned the next portion of the year in monthly chunks based on Betsy's experience. Typically fami-lies that go this route reflect on what's gone well in the year so far, and use what they've learned to plan the next block of time.

As she progressed through the year, Betsy decided to take advantage of her time off to do things she wouldn't have done in school. She took a writing class, volunteered at a children's hospital, waitressed at a local café, and enrolled in a gap program that took her to South America. However, even though it ended up working out for the best, Betsy does say the earlier you can start planning, the better. "It was stressful to plan in September rather than in June. Planning is key, as is figuring out and being honest about what you want," she says. "This was the one year I could do stuff that didn't have to be a resume builder, which allowed me to explore my interests more."

JUDGING PROGRAMS AND MAKING A DECISION

When you've narrowed down a few options and pin-pointed the important must-haves, it's time to pick up the phone. Because all gap year programs are vastly different, it's hard to standardize what differenti-ates a "good" program from a "bad" one. Looking at

AGA-accredited programs is a great place to start, but don't disqualify a program that's not accredited; there are plenty of top-notch companies that may not have the staff or bandwidth to go through the lengthy and costly accreditation process. Further, different educational bodies may accredit some programs, while many others simply choose not to be accredited.

For example, Dynamy, which was founded in 1969, is one of the country's oldest gap year programs. It also chooses not to be accredited by the AGA. "Since we have such a long history, and a solid foundation within the gap year community, we definitely have our own legs to stand on in terms of what we do and how we do it," says Cheng. "We're also not international, so a lot of what's laid out by the AGA doesn't even apply to us."

She says that in some cases, any type of accreditation should be taken with a grain of salt. "We're breaking the mold on education, so having someone define what a gap year program needs to be doesn't always make sense. Are there certain standards such as safety and support that need to be considered? Absolutely, but gap year is transforming education, so it's hard to say that your gap year must fit into these set criteria."

To illustrate, she says, "If I picked eight colleges and

said, 'These are the best eight colleges out of the thousands that are out there,' those eight may not fit certain students. And it's not because they're bad colleges, it's because maybe those students are thinking outside the box more."

The difference between a good program and a bad one could be as simple as whether or not it meets your child's needs, so accredited or not, aligning interests should be the main focus.

Available programs span the full spectrum and can get incredibly niche. To start, ask your child broad questions, like whether they want to travel, volunteer, intern, discover a passion, or interact with animals. Some gap year programs are tailored to specific skills. As I mentioned, you can explore these options through Google, by browsing on GoOverseas. com, or by working with an educational consultant familiar with gap years. For example, one gapper who played lacrosse in high school entertained the idea of teaching the sport to kids in Costa Rica. Another earned his SCUBA certification and took on a conservation role that monitored the health of coral reefs in Australia.

While every program is different, Knight says the most successful ones share a few common traits. He suggests asking these questions:

- *Do they have a solid risk-management plan? A good organization should be willing to share this plan with you.*

- *What are their admission protocols? Who do they admit? How do they select students?*

- *Who's on staff? Who is the student spending time with on a daily basis? Ask for reviews and bios, then look up the team leaders on social media. Familiarizing yourself with the staff is a good way to gauge potential outcomes.*

From there, it's all about feeling out the program directors and poking around to make an educated decision. Nothing is ever perfect, but going with your gut can go a long way toward making the right choice. It may also help you to speak with other parents and students who have graduated from a program. If names and numbers of past attendees aren't provided, ask the program to send a few your way.

At the end of the day, this is worth repeating: the right decision is what's right for your child, their interests, and their goals. That's numero uno, so don't be swayed by an expensive or international program if your child would gain more from a backwoods camping trip the next state over.

JUMPING IN WITH BOTH FEET

Congrats! You've found a program or designed a self-directed gap year that matches with your child's interests, and he or she is ready to get going. What's next?

Cassandra Tomkin, Chief Operating Officer for the international volunteer program Cross-Cultural Solutions, says six to nine months before the gap year begins is a good time to start preparing. If you're already past that mark, don't fret. Many families join gap year programs on much shorter notice.

The length of time available will dictate how quickly your child will need to get up to speed on prep materials. You can expect a good program to give your family reading matter, introduce you to program directors, share tidbits about the country's culture if your child is going abroad, and generally get everyone excited about what's to come.

As a parent, you may notice subtle changes in your child as the reality of the decision takes hold. "You really start the program when you enroll because it shifts your awareness immediately," says Carlton Rounds. "I tell students to set a Google alert for the country they're going to because every time something comes up, they'll get an email. That way when you get in-country and someone brings up a current event, the student can say, 'I read about that.'"

"The experience is so much richer if students come in with a little knowledge and understanding," adds Tomkin. "We want everyone to learn a little about the culture and history, and to think in advance about things like culture shock."

That said, don't allow yourself to get too carried away. Any parent with teenagers knows that getting overly excited about something is the fastest way to turn your kid off from it. Sarah Persha says she guides parents to not be overly amplified in their interest: "I invite parents who are interested to learn about the sites, the country, the language, but not to overshadow their child's preparedness."

Asking questions that trigger your child's interest to learn more, and then down playing your intensity, is important. You can say things like: "Did you know the language you're going to be speaking actually had its origins in the country next door?" or "Did you know they celebrate this festival and you're going to be there during that day?"

As a parent, you should also pay attention to your child's excitement level and how he or she is preparing. If your child is asking you to over-function—maybe they're not packing their bags or reading their materials— you have a problem, because that's a dependency. If you find that happening, you should have an honest discussion with your teen about how they're feeling, why they aren't taking an active role in the prep, and whether or not a gap year is the right choice. Chances are the lack of excitement is a sign of something bigger that needs to be addressed sooner rather than later. Further on, I'll discuss students who should not take a gap year in more detail.

ASK YOURSELF:

- Am I overwhelming my child by talking about the next step too much?

- Am I encouraging my child to do his/her own research?

- Is my child excited about the idea of a gap year?

- What does my child really like to do?

- What aspects are non-negotiables in my agreeing to a gap year?

- Am I doing it all for my child? Is my child asking me to do everything for him or her?

ASK YOUR CHILD:

- What sounds good to you? What do you like?

- What would you like to do this year?

- Rank the following in order of importance to you: fun, volunteer work, education, travel.

5: BANG-UPS, BRUISES, AND THINGS THAT GO BUMP IN THE NIGHT

"In the old days, all we had to worry about was sex, drugs, and rock and roll. That sounds simplistic now because the stakes have been raised."

– Linda Morgan, parent, grandparent, and parenting author

Sending your child off into the great unknown is probably one of the scariest feelings you'll encounter as a parent. That's why it's only natural that issues of safety and supervision come up in every conversation about gap years. The world is a scary place, and few countries function the way America does.

However, it's also important to remember that the media plays a big role in disseminating travel horror stories, and that the vast majority of students who leave home never encounter any serious issues. Though terrible things can happen anywhere—at home or abroad—there are steps you can take to help safeguard your teen before he or she leaves.

The first priority when we're talking safety should be to define the level of exploration you feel comfortable with. Linda Morgan says she's "right there" as the paranoid parent and recommends you figure out where you draw your own personal line. "I think that because of the media we are all alarmists at some level, and we think things are scarier than they really are. On the other hand, you have to be comfortable, so it's an individual thing."

Sarouhan says Interim often recommends students join a program first, even if they plan to travel alone later in the year. "If a student doesn't engage a professional organization, it's important to recognize that it is the student who will not only have to assess whatever risks are in an environment—whether that's traveling abroad or going off into the wilderness—but they're also going to have to manage that risk."

He continues: "If I were a parent, I would really want to be engaged in a conversation with my child about goals, helping them to develop the skills, and talking to them about the basic things: 'What happens when you have to go through customs and immigration? What are you going to do to keep yourself safe hailing a cab, even to go from the airport to your hotel? How are you going to approach going out at night in a city that you don't know? How are you going to keep your money and your body safe? What is the protocol that we're going to have together, as a family, about how frequently we're going to check in? And ultimately, what are the consequences if that doesn't happen?'"

If your teen is pushing to take a gap year independent of a program, you'd be wise to heed Sarouhan's earlier advice about identifying a mentor on the ground—someone in the community where your child wants to stay who would be in contact with you and watch over your teen, providing guidance in their choices and decisions. Perhaps this person would be a boss at a job placement, a homestay mother or father in the village, or a relative of yours who lives nearby.

After you've defined the boundaries, making sure the basics for international travel are accounted for is paramount. This includes getting up-to-date on all necessary vaccinations, purchasing travel insurance, checking the state of conflict in the country or city where your child will be staying, and talking to your teen about how to identify common dangers like predators and pickpockets. You should also register your son or daughter with the State Department before they go, and with the U.S. Embassy once they get in-country.

The Centers for Disease Control website has a comprehensive list of vaccine recommendations broken up by country, as well as danger warning levels, illness prevention tips, and information about food, water, and road safety. Additionally, every state has a Department of Health that's available to answer questions surrounding national and international travel. For an easy guide, see the links to these resources on my website at andreawien.com/gapyears.

For the first part of her gap year, Sophie Abo joined up to follow the Mekong River through China, Laos, and Cambodia with the program Where There Be Dragons. She says along with educating her about the culture and ecology of the region, the structure set the tone and pace for the rest of her year. It also armed her with valuable skills that enabled her to travel independently later on: "I wouldn't have been able to do the second part of the year if I hadn't done the program first. It taught me things, like how to get from one city to the next over land, and how to keep track of my stuff so I wouldn't lose my passport. I learned how to be a traveler, not a tourist."

VETTING A PROGRAM'S LEVEL OF CARE

Most times when families speak with an educational consultant or choose an accredited program, they're reassured that they're selecting from the safest possible programs. But even when a program isn't accredited, or when you're researching on your own, it's still possible to vet out safety concerns with staff. Asking questions around the structure of the program, the faculty, the admissions process, and the program rules will give you a good idea about the level of care and supervision.

When Shelly Cruze was initially weighing gap year options with her daughter Rebecca, cost was the main concern. But through the process, Shelly realized she was even more concerned about safety. She thought about how she would feel if Rebecca was in a foreign country and she was at home without total confidence in the program. "That just wasn't acceptable," she told me. "In the end, I'm glad we didn't mess around choosing a program, particularly when there was the earthquake in Nepal. I worried a lot while she was gone."

Shelly's fears are warranted. Though Rebecca wasn't near the Nepali earthquake, gappers Sophie Abo and Lucy Buckman were. Luckily, the girls were safe, but had they not learned the travel ropes earlier in the year, there could have been a lot more panic during the disaster.

When we talk about safety, it's not all about earth-shattering dangers like a natural disaster or a terrorist attack. Even smaller issues can derail a less experienced traveler. For example, on one gap trip, a stray dog bit a program guide. Luckily, the guide spoke the language, knew what he had to do, and found medical attention right away. A completely unforeseen circumstance like this can come up at any time, and if there's not someone there who's experienced and knows the lay of the land, problems can arise.

Selecting a gap program supervised by an experienced adult, who will be right there with the kids, boots on the ground, gives many parents a sense of reassurance. Depending on the itineraries and activities, programs may send guides from the student's home country, while others choose to enlist the help of country locals who speak the language, know the community, and are familiar with the customs and culture. It's important to know who will be with your child day-in and day-out, so do your due diligence in asking about the training and experience of any staff.

Most programs also institute a strong set of rules to help keep students safe. Rebecca was in a program that didn't allow partying, something her mom was insistent on before they signed up. "There are a lot of people who go to Thailand to party," says Shelly. "Rebecca said there was a lot of opportunity to drink if she wanted to, but she knew the program directors were very serious about enforcing the zero-tolerance policy."

No partying was also a test for Rebecca to see if she could stay true to herself, remain focused, and be there for the right reasons. "She was very proud of what she accomplished on the trip as far as learning more about herself and building confidence. She feels very empowered," says Shelly.

Gap programs like Carpe Diem, the program Rebecca took part in, have a contract that every gapper is required to sign at the start of their experience. In it, gappers agree to refrain from alcohol, drugs, and risky or harmful behaviors. They also agree to challenge themselves, treat others with respect, and abide by all group decisions. "We call our rules the Sacred Six, and we are very serious about them," says Drew Edwards. "We absolutely mean what we say, and every single year we send students home for violating the policies."

The programs that restrict alcohol in-country aren't doing so to limit the students' fun. Preventable injuries are the leading cause of death and disability in travelers in general, and alcohol increases the likelihood of an accident. "Drinking is easily one of the most dangerous preventable situations students can put themselves in while abroad, and it's an added liability that we're unwilling to take on," says Edwards. "From a sheer safety perspective, we are incredibly serious about that."

Even parents who ethically may not have an issue with drinking told me that removing it from the equation during the gap year was constructive. Instead of blurring or dulling the interactions, not drinking allowed their children to be fully present, to reflect, and to explore more safely.

For students who chose to do self-directed gap years, drinking was a personal decision, often based on where they were traveling. When Lucy and Sophie journeyed through India and Nepal alone in the spring of 2015, they consciously made a choice not to drink. "In terms of being smart, we just thought it wasn't worth it," Lucy says.

The level of individual care students may receive during a gap year can reveal itself in the application process. Independent educational consultant Diane Geller says that when she's vetting a program for a client, she draws the parallel to customer service: "If you're caught in a telephone loop without really feeling that anyone is listening or paying attention to your inquiry, do you really want to buy the product? I think, 'If they aren't kind to me as a potential customer, what are they going to be like later?'"

Selectivity on the part of the program can sometimes, but not necessarily, indicate a higher level of care. Pia Wong says, for Riley, it was important to choose a program that wasn't pay-to-play. "We wanted to make sure the kids were doing the program because they wanted to be doing it, and not as some sort of disciplinary action, or because they were forced into it." A selective application process was important to Pia because she felt it would weed out the kids who were applying for the wrong reasons.

Program selectivity may help weed out anyone who shouldn't be doing a particular gap year, but that's not to say all programs with selective screening processes are good. Neither are all programs bad that allow any teen to join. The important thing is that the program is a good fit for your particular teen, and that you feel comfortable with the level of attention he or she will receive during their time away. Different families require different levels of care.

THE SPECTRUM OF GAP YEAR SUPERVISION

I asked Sarouhan about the different extremes in gap program supervision. He says that on one end, there are fully facilitated experiences where students join a community of peers with group leaders, mentors, and teachers who are essentially with the group twenty-four hours a day, seven days a week. Though this may sound overbearing, most gap programs are looking to foster independence, so group leaders are trained to back off a bit when students have shown the skills necessary to thrive in the new environment.

"Leaders ensure that students are given the chance to practice those skills, make mistakes, and learn. As the program progresses, leaders will ultimately start giving students much greater levels of independence, and a say in designing their experience," Sarouhan says.

Similarly, some volunteer placements have incredibly high levels of infrastructure: "There are programs that will meet each volunteer at the airport, drive them back to a site where all volunteers live, with separate men's and women's dorms, feed them nourishing food, and provide private transport back and forth to really well-oiled volunteer projects with onsite supervisors," says Sarouhan. "And of course, these projects have very detailed plans for what happens if a student gets sick or injured. They're going to be taken to the best Westernized medical care, with English-speaking translators, that's available in that region."

At the other extreme, supervision and support can be virtually non-existent in a gap year, if that's what a family decides they're comfortable with. Sarouhan says he worked with one young woman who went on assignment in Buenos Aires with a small non-profit organization: "She was met at the airport by a Spanish-speaking driver and driven out to a remote community the same day. Her family knew where she was, but it wasn't really locatable on a map. She was introduced to her homestay mother right then and there on the spot," he says.

"The driver told her, 'If you have an emergency, or if you need anything, here's my number. Otherwise, I'll be back to pick you up in three months.' And this young woman stayed, kind of Peace Corps-style without the training, in this rural village with her homestay mother for three months while working at the local school. Her supervisor was the principal of the school, her main point of contact was her homestay mom, and she did not see other volunteers for the whole time."

Obviously, this is an example of an extremely low level of infrastructure, and while most students don't desire that, you should be ready to have honest and open conversations with your son or daughter if they are pushing hard for a highly independent gap year that's light on adult support and protection.

MAKING IT SCARIER THAN IT SHOULD BE

Even when planning has been meticulous, last-minute stress can still send parents into a tailspin. "Right before he left, there were all these news reports about child refugees from South America, and I'm thinking, 'What am I doing?'" says Pia Wong, whose son Riley traveled to South America.

To calm her fears, she kept reminding herself that Riley had insurance, and the program they chose had a great reputation. "Any time I had a question, the responses I received from the staff were very solid," she says. "Things go wrong, but I felt like there were enough measures in place to keep him safe. Plus, sometimes with travel you have to take a leap of faith—you can't be worried about all the things that could go wrong."

Rob Spach, whose son Christopher did a self-directed gap year, says he encourages parents to trust that their son or daughter is going to be able to deal with what they're confronted with, and not to allow fear to drive their decisions. "We're a culture that, for whatever reason, has imbibed a lot of fear. Because of that, we're really reticent to do things that a gap year sometimes means doing," he says.

On the front end, be wise about the situation your child is going into, and help them think from a positive perspective—that the adventure will stretch them but not be flat-out dangerous. "You'd be crazy to send your child to a gap year in Syria," says Rob. "That would be stupid. But to send them someplace that's really unfamiliar, that just *feels* scary to the family, is different. And you have to trust your son's or daughter's ability to cope without you and make decisions."

From where O'Shea sits as an administrator at FSU, he sees more opportunities for things to go wrong in college than in traveling abroad: "There's more incentive to do the binge drinking that happens so often in social events on college campuses. People sometimes have a fear of the unknown, and that fear leads them to make hasty generalizations about what it's like, or to mischaracterize the actual risk of living in a foreign country."

In the end, it all comes down to doing your homework and arriving at a place where you're comfortable with sending your child away. Read reviews, talk to people, and don't hesitate to keep pushing until your questions get answered. "The stakes are high," says mom, Shelly Cruze. "If they travel, your kid is in a foreign country, and you have to feel confident with what's going on."

She adds: "I do wish I hadn't worried quite so much, but that was just my own thing. I was just so anxious."

ASK YOURSELF:

- Am I being honest about the level of independence I'm okay with?

- Am I being overly paranoid?

- Have I properly vetted the safety procedures within a program?

- Am I confident in the responses I've received to my questions?

- Have I had an honest and open conversation with my child about how they'll respond to social pressures abroad?

- Based on maturity level, how much supervision does my child really require?

ASK YOUR CHILD:

- Are you nervous about being able to turn down drinking or other risky behavior?

- How would you react in a dangerous situation? (Suggest a few scenarios.)

- What, to you, constitutes an emergency?

- What level of independence do you expect to have during your gap year?

6 : TELLING GRANDMA AND NEIGHBOR NORM

"This is a reality that many parents have to face. But before they even think about what they might tell someone else, they need to fully believe in this themselves without feeling shamed or embarrassed."

– Drew Edwards, Executive Director, Carpe Diem Education

Forget baseball, basketball, and football. College admissions and the race for the Ivy Leagues should be re-classified as America's national sport. The competition to get into a good school starts before preschool. For many of my friends in big cities, it shockingly starts when the baby is still in utero. I remember a friend calling me up a few years back, asking me to provide a reference for their then-four-*month*-old daughter. They were practically pulling their hair out while putting her through a rigorous preschool screening process.

In her book, *How to Raise an Adult: Break Free of the Overparenting Trap and Prepare Your Kid for Success*, Julie Lythcott-Haims, former freshman dean at Stanford University, tells the story of how she and her husband drove their two-day-old baby to a prestigious preschool in Silicon Valley to drop off an application form. She explains that they didn't want to seem "uncommitted." Something in our culture has gone seriously awry when a mother's C-section wounds haven't even scabbed over before she's spiraling into a panic about the future academic standing of her newborn.

When a child decides to hit pause for a gap year, it can feel in some ways like a failure to both the student and the parent. Being honest with yourself about your own feelings will be critical in how you communicate the experience to others. Are you really behind this decision, or are you trying to compensate for your perceived lack of something in your child?

Talking with your son or daughter about why they want to do this can help to shine a flashlight into your head. The reason your child wants to take a gap year is most likely not to goof off or waste time. "It's also not about being lost, which is something we so commonly hear," says Edwards. "It's about finding out more about yourself. It's about challenging yourself mentally, physically, emotionally, and culturally. It's about having a broader global perspective and expanding your horizons beyond that which you have seen and experienced thus far. And it's about being a better human, and certainly a better student, for having done it."

Even once all immediate family members feel comfortable with the decision, outsiders who don't believe in straying off the traditional course are still an omnipresence. In a perfect world, everyone would honor an individual's decision to do what's best for them. But in reality, we live in a hyper-competitive society—and the claws are out for battle.

"There's this sense of 'I have to beat my neighbor, or I have to excel, because it's not just about me, it's about winning,'" says psychologist Karen Bridbord. "But winning what? Winning the war but losing the peace? So you got into an Ivy League that's actually not a good fit for you. Are you happy? Are you productive? Are you getting to where you want to be?"

OUTSIDERS RESPOND

Holly Swartz says initially she wasn't overly enthusiastic about the gap year, but she's come around after seeing how it's altered her daughter's perspective. "It's changed the way she sees the world, and that's a great gift to be able to give your child," she says. "I'm quite enthusiastic about the gap year now. In our case, this wasn't a kid who wasn't ready for college, but instead a kid who wanted to see the world and expand her horizons."

When Swartz first started telling people about her daughter's decision to go gap, she says she encountered divergent responses. On one hand, there were a group of cheerleaders who were incredibly excited and supportive. "Mostly that's a group who's experienced the world and are in favor of expansive world experiences," she explains.

On the other side, there were naysayers who were appalled by Swartz's decision to let her daughter postpone formalized education. To those people, she tried to gently explain that this experience was something that would be important to her daughter over a lifetime.

Gapper Betsy Morgan had a similar experience when she had to abruptly leave Harvard after falling ill in the first two weeks, then recovering and spending the remainder of the school year in a gap program. "I come from a community where everyone goes to college, so one of the biggest negatives of the gap experience for me was the stigma attached to it. When I decided to come home from Harvard, it felt like I'd failed because you either go to college or you've somehow messed up."

She says that because the concept of gap years is a foreign one for many people, it became more and more draining to keep explaining her reasons for college deferment. "I wish there was more flexibility in what people's plans are after high school, and more acceptance of the idea that a gap year can actually be more helpful than going immediately to school."

For students who don't have an illness or similarly "understandable" answers to queries about why they're taking a break, the conversation can be even more uncomfortable. "I'm a university professor, I'm half-Asian, and I grew up with a tiger mom, so [other people's] perception is way more important [to me] than I'd like to admit," says Pia Wong. "For me, it was important that my son applied to school, so we could have the conversation with other families that he's going to college, he's just doing it in a year instead of now. Having a college plan was very important."

TEMPORARILY OPTING OUT OF THE RACE

If your family has decided that a gap year is the right move, there's plenty of data to support that you're not ruining your child's future, and, in fact, are helping your student to excel in a healthier way.

In a study of over seven-hundred gappers, 73% said their experience increased their readiness for university. Students also reported higher GPAs after their gap year, and a study by Middlebury College found that the boost in academic performance lasted all four undergraduate years.

Time off isn't only a luxury for liberal arts students. National statistics show that nearly half of medical school-minded students are taking at least one gap year, according to David Verrier, Director of the Office of Pre-Professional Programs and Advising at Johns Hopkins University in Baltimore. For students at research institutions like Johns Hopkins, the percentage is even higher: up to 60% of students take a year or more off.

While it can be hard to field questions from friends and extended family day-in and day-out, arming yourself with statistics and information like this can put you in a good position to educate others.

"Part of this competition is the idea that everybody has to go to the absolute hardest college to get into, and there's really no data that those kids are more successful," says parenting author Linda Morgan. "It's a myth that everyone has to do that. But when you see your friends doing it, it looks like you have to jump on that bandwagon, and that's part of the problem. The truth is that 80% to 90% of really good colleges in the country are accessible, and if you're a good enough student, you'll get into one of them." With nearly three thousand four-year colleges in the country, it would be crazy to think Morgan isn't right.

ASKING BETTER QUESTIONS

Along with realizing why the competition exists, it can be helpful to reframe the college question entirely. "I think instead of 'Is Susie going to Yale?' the question should be, 'Is Susie really happy?'" says psychologist Karen Bridbord.

It's true that people talk about the "accomplishments" of students while simultaneously disregarding their mental health completely: "How many perfectionistic females are straight-A students and great athletes, crossing their t's and dotting their i's, but they have eating disorders?" Bridbord asks. "To me, that's a reflection of their emotional life."

"Children quickly learn that they have to 'be' and perform a certain way in order to be loved—or they make that association, even if it's not necessarily true," she explains. "They feel like they will get rewarded and loved if they are perfect, whatever that definition of perfect is."

A child's emotional life is birthed in the home, but competition today is magnified in every area of a student's life. And once students lose themselves in the process of seeking approval, all sorts of issues—from eating disorders to drug use—arise.

"This very rigid kind of experience unfolds where they're doing all of these things, but those things aren't necessarily what that person wants or needs," says Bridbord. "And yet the pursuit of love is the most important."

In our society, a connection to the self and the nurturing of a strong emotional life is something we seem to have lost track of when we hopped on the

high-performance escalator. Consider how powerful it is to use your child's intended gap year as an
excuse to boast about their emotional intelligence and
self-awareness instead of taking an apologetic attitude
with friends and family. Your child will feel your pride
and trust, and that will fuel their self-esteem and further their maturation.

GAP AS A BADGE OF HONOR

Bragging rights aren't something Shelly Cruze
expected to earn when her daughter first set out for
her gap year. But by the end, she was able to say, "Yeah,
my kid went off and did this amazing thing. I didn't
expect that I was going to be able to brag about it."

Cruze's other daughter also strayed a bit from the traditional course when she postponed the beginning of
her junior year in college for an internship in Italy. "As
a parent, I'm really proud of both of them for their for-
titude, drive, and determination. And I'm proud that
they're going out and grabbing some of these experiences, not being so wedded to the tradition of how
things should be done."

When I asked one gapper's dad about what he took
away from his son's gap experience, he told me, "Just
that I have a really cool son."

ASK YOURSELF:

- Am I completely behind this?

- If not, what's holding me back from fully supporting this decision?

- Am I responding to a social stigma or to my own fear?

- How will I respond when someone asks me about my child's plans?

- How can I help to prepare my child for any negative reactions?

ASK YOUR CHILD:

- Why do you want to do a gap year?

- Why is this important to you?

- Are you happy?

- What do you hope to learn through this experience?

- Are you scared or nervous about what lies ahead?

7: A SCAVENGER HUNT FOR SUCCESS

"It's said that the best parents give their children roots and wings. You give them roots so they understand home, their foundation, and the values that you've built. Then you give them wings so they soar on their own into a wider universe."

– Mindy Nierenberg, Senior Director, Tisch College Programs

In my family, success means something completely different to me than it does to my mom. My mother grew up in Romania during Communism, immigrating at fourteen with her parents and brother to Canton, Ohio. As a child, she dreamt of financial security and valued nice things, so when she married my father and landed a job at the local hospital, she was well on her way to meeting her definition of success. I was born when she was twenty-four, and my parents built their first home at the age of twenty-six. More successful steps achieved.

During my childhood, I was the lucky recipient of the fruits of my parents' success. I rarely wanted for new clothes or toys. I lived in a great house and had a loving family. When I went to college, I continued to propagate my mother's idea of what success looked like. I was following a path that she agreed with. But when I turned nineteen, I decided to take time away from school and move to New York City for an internship.

"No. You can't go," my mother told me. When I asked why, she said she was worried I wouldn't go back to finish my degree. She was concerned about safety. And she felt an obligation as my parent to make sure I made decisions that would keep me on the path to success.

The problem wasn't that my mom didn't believe in me. The problem was that our ideas of success were different—and still are. To her, success means stability and safety. To me, success means taking risks, calculated chaos, and filling my life with one adventure after another. Where my mother values security and routine, I value autonomy and a manageable level of uncertainty. Where she puts a premium on material possessions, I prefer to gather experiences.

There's nothing wrong with either of our definitions of success, and plenty of people will relate to both. The issue is that many parents don't understand how their child's idea of success could vary so greatly from their own. After all, you raised them!

Ultimately, I ended up going to New York for the internship. And when I returned to school, I realized right away that I wanted to get back to New York as quickly as possible. In turn, my dedication to graduating skyrocketed, and I ended up completing college a year earlier than anticipated.

Still, our different concepts of success are something my mother and I have struggled with for years, and it's not an issue that's easy to sweep under the rug. It's the same issue that causes so many artists to end up in law school—they're searching for their parents' approval by bowing to their parents' definition of success.

"Kids want their parents' approval," says Bridbord. "It's an innate desire. I've never met a person who said, 'Ah, doesn't matter to me.' Even if they think they don't need it, it's still very nice to have it. And the big-kept secret is that parents want their kids' approval, too."

WHEN INDIVIDUATING IS PAINFUL

This lesson isn't an easy one for my family, and chances are, it's not easy for yours. To fully allow your child to individuate takes immense amounts of strength and self-awareness—both in your relationship with your child and within yourself.

It's not a process that happens overnight, but a good place to start is coming to terms with the fact that your child is a separate being from you. "Parents should understand that though we bring our children into the world, or we nurture children in cases of adoption, they are not extensions of us. They are separate, and we need to remember and have a respect for that reality," says Bridbord.

The process of individuating starts as early as the moment the child comes out of the womb. Before that, there's no sense of differentiation between the self and the other. But then, Bridford says, you get to the terrible twos. "And why is it so terrible? Because the parent is saying, 'no, no, no' all the time, but the child is thinking, '*No*. This is what *I* want.' These are the first signs of blatant individuation."

In the case of your adolescent child, it comes down to honoring your differences, as opposed to finding them threatening or scary. Parents are trying to protect their kids, when they should really just be allowing them to have their feelings.

PARENTAL SCAFFOLDING

The poet Maya Angelou said, "Success is liking your-self, liking what you do, and liking how you do it." Sounds easy enough, but in practice, success can be infinitely harder to nail down. And for your child, it's almost impossible to figure out what success looks like without some healthy guidance from you.

That's where the concept of scaffolding can help. It's not all about giving kids what they want all the time. "That's not what I'm promoting," says Bridbord. "There are times when your kid might think they don't like something, or they may feel some anxiety. But how many of us have felt anxiety, and then done something and realized, 'Geez, I can really do this?' Scaffolding is where you provide the least amount of support you can while providing enough support so the kid can do it and learn from it."

Obviously the connection between scaffolding on a building and scaffolding in a relationship is strong: the temporary structure holds up the building until it's able to stand on its own. The end result of scaffolding your child is that they are able to stand on their own, to live their life independent of you.

Along with teaching kids, scaffolding can also help when it comes to decision-making. Parents can scaffold by asking kids open-ended questions like, "What do you think about this?" The key then is really listening to their answers.

"We try to teach kids how to listen, but as parents, we need to listen to our children because they have messages to share as they are learning about who they are as people," says Bridbord. "Parents may think, 'I know better.' In some regards, you may know better, but your child is connected with herself deeply and should be encouraged to connect with herself."

SKILLS, INTERESTS, AND VALUES

When helping a young person figure out what to do with their life, it's not just their interests we need to pay attention to, but a combination of interests *and* values. For example, if someone values creativity and flexibility, a finance degree and a traditional role in corporate probably won't fill their bucket of success. But if their value lies in making a lot of money, then a high-powered career track could make sense.

A good career counselor knows that interests and skills aren't enough. Counselors have to also look at the values because the value of a job and what a job provides is a context that can't be ignored. This is also where the self-awareness piece comes in, because values often correlate with a person's strengths.

To start parsing together what your child's values are, it's important to expose him or her to a variety of different experiences they may not get in school. If they haven't had an opportunity to explore prior to this stage of life, the gap year can have an especially profound impact.

In the case of Betsy Morgan, that's exactly what happened. Devastated by having to leave campus after getting sick, Betsy turned her attention to how she would spend her year off. Once she felt better, she began volunteering at the local children's hospital, and a few months later, she started waitressing. But when it came time for the second part of the year, the idea of a gap program crept into the picture.

It wasn't something Betsy had even considered in her previous track, but when she found a program that combined service, education, and adventure travel, her interest piqued, and she signed on. "For the first few weeks in South America, it was a hard adjustment. There was culture shock and homesickness, and I wanted to be in college like all my friends. Also traveling with strangers is a weird experience," she says.

"But after I normalized, it was the best experience I've ever had. I learned so much in terms of life experience—how to find my way when I was lost, how to get directions in an unfamiliar city or book a hostel. Those things seem inconsequential at the time, but it really added up to make me a more confident and together person. I learned in a way that was so different than how I'd always learned."

Through her time off, Betsy's values—her idea of success—solidified. Rather than return to Harvard, she decided Washington University in St. Louis was a better fit. And instead of blindly diving headfirst into a general business degree, she realized through her volunteer work with the children's hospital that she valued working in healthcare. Now, she's adjusted her coursework to explore the medical field, and she's considering adding a minor in international business because of her travel experiences.

LEARNING BY DOING

Betsy's experience isn't unique. According to data from the American Gap Association, 77% of students who take a gap year report that their experience helped them find purpose in their life, in addition to impacting their career decision.

Along with helping to determine the next step, a gap year also provides students with the opportunity to get hands-on with their learning. Exposure to experiences and even chance encounters are critical to a student's direction. Without exposure, it's very difficult to choose something they don't know exists.

The experience also doesn't have to be 100% positive to be illuminating. Independent educational consultant Diane Geller says that even menial tasks can help students frame their futures: "If a student isn't ready for college, or is not ready to be away from home, getting a part-time job can go a long way. If through that experience they learn, 'I don't want to do retail' or 'I don't want to deliver pizza,' then there's a lot to be said for that realization."

As a society, we place too much pressure on getting to the finish line, but in reality, it's in the processing that learning happens. You don't learn geometry or chemistry just by reading about it. You learn through the process of practicing it, experiencing it, and sometimes, failing at it.

FAILURE AS AN OPTION

Recently I met a young woman in her mid-twenties at a friend's loft in New York. We were having a conversation about the "modern man" and what role presence and meditation play in creating a healthier society. At the end of the discussion, the woman told me she had found meditation after hitting "rock bottom." She said she'd gone through her entire life without experiencing failure. Born in Manhattan to an upper-class family, all of her disappointments had been mitigated by her parents. She had breezed through adolescence, attended a top-tier university, moved across the country to San Francisco, and secured a string of successful jobs post-graduation.

After a few years, she took a position in Washington, D.C. The job turned out to be a disaster, and her feeling of security vanished when she made the decision to leave almost immediately upon arrival. She moved back in with her parents, barely able to function because of the turn of events.

As I listened to her, I kept thinking she was about to

launch into a story about how she'd fallen in with the wrong crowd or maxed out every credit card. But she didn't. Her "failure" was nothing more than an easily corrected wrong turn. Her "rock bottom" didn't really cost her much other than a little additional stress, and I couldn't shake the feeling that her idea of the bottom was anything but.

In the story of every accomplished person, the road to success is paved with setbacks and major mistakes. Everyone from Bill Gates to Muhammad Ali talks about the power of failure, while business magazines and venture capitalists extol the virtues of "failing fast and failing often."

And yet, parents are more determined than ever to ensure their children don't fail. The consequences are disastrous. In the case of the young woman I just described, the fact that she'd never been allowed to fail made her first "failure" a cataclysmic event. Instead of dusting herself off and getting on with it, she'd crumbled under the pressure. Thankfully, she had sought out a healthy practice in meditation versus something more destructive.

When I hear stories like this, I find myself asking: Why are we so worried about letting kids fail? You want your child to be independent and resilient, but if you're not creating a culture where it's okay to fail, you're enabling the opposite. This is problematic across the board, but can be especially traumatic when a student gets on campus.

"A lot of Princeton students are used to being highly successful, certainly academically, but they're also often captains of their sports teams and presidents of their student governments," says Scott Leroy, Princeton's Bridge Year Associate Director. "When they get to Princeton, they're going to fail. It's inevitable because every student who comes to Princeton struggles in some respect. But when they immerse themselves in another culture where they don't speak the language, for example, it's hard to be polished and successful all the time. So having had this gap year experience prepares them for that failure to some extent."

Linda Morgan, parenting expert and author, says if parents step back, stop the constant fixing and rescuing, and allow their child to make their own decisions, that's powerful: "Maybe a gap year helps to foster that independence because they're doing something completely different that's theirs alone. They're getting to know themselves a little better in the process, and taking risks; not just academically, but socially, intellectually, emotionally."

THE IMPORTANCE OF REFLECTION

"Proximity is not insight," says Carlton Rounds, Director of Campus Engagement at Cross-Cultural Solutions. What he means is that simply *existing* in a new environment without any self-awareness or time to reflect on an experience does not translate to having an enlightening transformation.

Sarouhan agrees. He says of the core components that gap year professionals talk about, the level of insight and reflection present during time off is at the top of the list: "To any parent who is encouraging their son or daughter to go off to travel around the world, my question would be: what do you hope your child is actually going to get out of that experience? I ask that because we have to create context in order to actually have learning happen. Just because one has traveled to India doesn't mean you have a much deeper understanding of some of the major global issues we're facing around the world."

His comments hit close to home. On my own trip to India in the spring of 2015, I met two gappers from the U.K. They planned to travel for six months, skipping across Southeast Asia before setting off for university in the fall. As one does in the digital age, we exchanged

Instagram names, so I was able to track their progress and peek in on their adventures across the continent.

Of course, social media is not a substitute for real-life interaction, but as I watched their trip through my phone screen, I was awestruck by how little they seemed to glean from their time away. Between partying in Bali, Thailand, India, and Laos, with very little time spent interacting with the culture (aside from the bartender at the pool), they seemed to have missed out on the magic of what travel can provide. To bookmark their trip, they posted one final, drunken picture. The caption read: "Eight countries later and we're still not cultured."

I grimaced. Travel is a privilege and a great opportunity for honing life skills that can't be learned on your home soil. But when travel is disrespected and minimized to which fruity drink tastes better in which country, I fear gappers miss the mark. I have no doubt these two ladies had a blast traversing the globe, shot glass in one hand, camera in the other. And I'm not discounting that there were probably a few undocumented learning experiences along the way.

But unfortunately—without a vision, plan, or time for reflection—a gap year can turn into nothing more than an excuse to escape school or drink oneself into self-indulgent oblivion. I'd argue that when that happens, a gap year isn't any better than a hazy and wasted (pun intended) freshman year in a college dorm. When the view blurs after a few drinks, the scenery seldom matters.

If you're looking for gap programs, you'd be best served to find one that values time spent reflecting and allowing students to stop and focus on what they're doing. At Cross-Cultural Solutions, program directors who have a deep understanding of both the social issues of the community and of culture shock lead sessions that encourage students to reflect, both as a group and individually.

Those same directors also act as mentors, creating an environment where informal discussion is encouraged. For example, in Morocco, volunteers may spend time talking about the perceptions of Islam or the role of women in society. "A big part of a program director's day, every single day, is making time to have really deep conversations with volunteers. Not only is he acting as a mentor, but he also views it as an investment in his community to share his culture," says Cassandra Tomkin.

If your child isn't joining a program, or if the program you've chosen doesn't provide structured time for reflection, it's still possible to make reflection a priority. The key is to start small, as pushing reflection onto your child will most likely only make them less interested.

Mention the idea of journaling or blogging during the gap year as a way to keep an account of the experiences. You can also prompt them to think about life by starting conversations where you ask your child to tell you something that had meaning for him or her in the course of the last day. Inviting your son or daughter to recall an emotion can help to train their mind for reflection. What you're really after, through encouraging reflection, is establishing a strong sense of self and encouraging them to hone their positive self-talk skills.

Ideally, asking questions will prompt students to begin to ask questions of themselves so they can get at the heart of what they did or didn't like about something. "Kids have a difficult time articulating this stuff," says Bridbord. "No one teaches us how to talk to ourselves, but we indirectly learn and internalize all sorts of messages. In the worst case, negative messages and judgment are internalized. But reflection is really a tool to develop a sense of self."

A reflection practice also aids in the development of discipline. I'm not talking about discipline like grounding or taking away the car keys, but a deeper sense of discipline that starts from the inside out.

At the Cleveland School for the Arts, Daniel Gray-Kontar teaches creative writing to teenagers and young adults. His classroom doesn't look like a typical classroom. Instead, students lounge on couches, and discussions revolve around philosophy, mindfulness and meditation, or the written word. He wants the space to feel safe, and his students start each day focusing on a candle—a practice that's meant to bring them into the present.

"What I try to teach young people is how to be present within yourself, how to be mindful of yourself, how to be mindful of your breath, how to meditate, how to think about what you need so you can think about what others need. When we begin to do this, we find that what we're actually teaching is discipline," says Gray-Kontar.

He continues: "This is important for our students because often the discipline they receive is punitive, and they're not really learning from that. But when they begin to learn how to be present within themselves, it's there that they begin to analyze why it is that they do the things that they do."

Through this discipline students grow confidence. Through confidence comes grit. And grit is one of those intangibles that experts say is a key piece to the puzzle of success.

"Grit is really the ability to continue even when things get tough. It's not throwing in the towel when you fail," says Bridbord. When your child feels like they're not good at something because they don't immediately succeed at it, that's a problem because they're unlikely to keep trying. "Children need to have the grit to endure through failure, so teaching grit and how to stick with something is important," Bridbord adds.

In a gap program, there are usually measures in place to make sure everyone is engaged with the process. But if your teen is on an independent gap year, it can be tough to monitor whether or not they're actively dialed into their experience. That's yet another reason Interim recommends joining a program first.

"It's really worthwhile for students to take more of a progression-based approach to independence, starting with a greater level of support where they're being nurtured by people who have experience, and then moving to much more independence later on in their year," says Sarouhan.

To illustrate, he compares the experience of a gap year to learning how to swim: "We don't take brand new swimmers to the deep end of the pool, and throw them in without any floatation, or without someone being there. It's the same thing."

WHEN A GAP YEAR DOESN'T FIT

While a gap year can benefit nearly everyone who takes one, there are a few instances where it might not be the best fit. If you and your child have never separated and have anxiety about the thought of being apart, you may find the gap experience a struggle. Be honest with yourself about the level of independence you're comfortable with, and understand that if you choose a program, it's not the staff's job to keep you updated constantly.

"The gap program is not going to stay in touch with the parents, because they're busy with the kids," says Sarah Persha. "The best gap programs might bulletin out: 'Hey, this is where we're at this week, and this is what they're doing.' I tell parents that if you're going to be anxious all the time, then pick a program where you can have more contact from both staff and student."

Another case where a gap year might not fit is if your child is passionate about school and continuing formal education without interruption. In that scenario, it's not the right time. "If the student loves school, then stick to what they love doing," says Ethan Knight, AGA's president. "The student will know when the time is right to try something else."

On the flip side, Sarouhan says students who haven't found their way in high school, or are really unmotivated in general, may not thrive during the gap year.

"There are many students who did not do well in high school who do well in gap year, and there are many students who don't know if they want to go to college who thrive in gap year, but it has to be a choice," he explains. "Gap year is not the easy path. It requires not only a tremendous amount of courage, but it also requires a student who is willing to put themselves through a pretty amazing period of growth."

He says that students who are not excited about a gap year, who are not invested in the experience, who don't see the potential for themselves, or who aren't willing to take the step out of their comfort zone shouldn't take a gap year. They're simply not ready.

One last scenario to consider is if your child has a

mental illness, such as an anxiety disorder, that may pose a disruption to their experience. When issues like homesickness don't go away because the student is either too anxious, or they're not emotionally stable enough to be there, then they aren't going to be able to learn. Persha says that's very rare, but she's had programs contact her and say, "This is beyond homesickness."

O'Shea says that he's seen students who want to take a gap year because they're trying to run away from something: "They think it's a cure for mental illness, or an eating disorder, for example. You have to be careful in those situations because as one veteran gap administrator told me, gap years have a way of bringing back old habits." That's because the gap year can be stressful at times, and when students are removed from their support group, they can feel isolated, which can cause issues to resurface.

While some programs have mental health specialists on staff to help stabilize students in the field, it's still imperative that you try to anticipate your child's needs. A gap year can be a great way to foster independence, and while homesickness is expected to some extent, understanding your child's mental state before sending them away from home is critical to their safety and ultimate happiness. Without this level of critical analysis, you're putting your child—and whomever else they encounter—at potential risk.

When we're dealing with mental illness, it's hard to make firm recommendations about when a gap year is most appropriate for a student's well being. If you have any questions around this issue, you should speak to a health care provider before sending your teen on a gap year, or look into programs like Summit, Soar, or the Crossroads Institute. These more therapeutic-based programs provide different levels of support for students who may not be ready to take a more main-stream gap year.

ASK YOURSELF:

- Does my child come to me for everything, or is he/she self-sufficient?

- Is my child a good critical thinker?

- Is my child a problem solver?

- Do I do things for my child that at their age they should be doing for themselves?

- If my child received a parking ticket, would they be capable of independently dealing with the situation?

- Am I teaching my child to be aware of their own feelings?

- Does my child feel comfortable making decisions?

ASK YOUR CHILD:

- If you received a parking ticket, how would you handle it? [Hint: if they answer, "call you," that's a red flag.]

- How do you feel about leaving home in the next year?

- What are your fears or concerns about finishing high school?

- What excites you about the next year?

- How do you know that you're successful?

- What makes you happy?

- What are your favorite activities?

- In an ideal world, how would you spend your time?

- If you could design the perfect day, what would it look like?

- What options are you aware of after high school graduation?

8 : BUT WHAT
ABOUT THE COST?

"Everyone who goes abroad can't be a white woman between the ages of eighteen and twenty-two because that's not what the U.S. is. I think if the gap movement really spreads out, and it is high quality, you're going to see some government help."

– Carlton Rounds, Director of Campus Engagement, Cross-Cultural Solutions

Parents often say that while they saved to send their child to college for four years, they most certainly did not save for an additional gap year. College is expensive, and for many, tacking on another year of $20,000 in travel expenses and fun isn't in the cards.

For the AGA, cost is one of the biggest hurdles to advancing the gap year movement. And while scholarships for gap years have started to spring up by generous donors who believe in the power of the gap, it's still—for many families—an expensive experience to justify.

So how can you possibly afford this? The programs themselves are a good place to start. Plenty of programs have scholarships in place to support students. In 2013 alone, AGA-affiliated organizations gave away almost $3 million. The AGA has also launched a network of individual scholarships called the "Back-a-Gapper" Program. At the time of this writing, there's one donor on board, but check back often to see if more opportunities have been added to the list.

Many of the programs also offer tuition reductions. While not every family will qualify, it won't hurt to inquire about whether your child is eligible. Additionally, programs will often work to customize a payment plan with you. By spreading out payments over six months, or the full year, many families find that the sticker shock is less palpable.

Non-profit organizations around the globe also offer scholarship dollars to traveling students. Projects like Carpe Mundi, for example, provide first-generation college students in the Portland, Oregon area the opportunity to apply for aid to join an educational gap program. Last spring, the organization sent eleven students on full rides, and in 2016, fourteen students will attend the program for free.

You can also check in with your local government and city council to see if there's any interest in setting up a scholarship fund for gap year students. Providing information, data points, and case studies like the ones outlined in this book can be useful in championing a positive response.

GOVERNMENT HELP

When I attended the first-ever gap year conference in May 2015, the topic of government financial aid was a hot-button issue. Unfortunately, as the representative from the State Department told us, students who aren't enrolled in a university during their gap year can't qualify for government assistance. However, the AGA is lobbying the U.S. government to make gap years eligible for financial aid dollars. Currently, AGA's president, Ethan Knight, says there are a few opportunities on the table that could make this possible as early as 2016.

Just because there isn't any current government assistance, that doesn't mean the government doesn't support gappers. In fact, the U.S. State Department just created its own branch to increase the number of students studying abroad. It's a huge initiative that the gap community is watching closely.

FREE OR LOW-COST PROGRAMS

Programs like AmeriCorps and City Year offer stipends to students in exchange for a year of service. Unlike other gap programs, students won't have the opportunity to tailor their experience specifically to themselves, but if your child's interests align with the missions of organizations like these, they can be a good fit.

Individual programs at the collegiate level, like those of the Tufts and Princeton bridge years, have also been established to democratize the gap experience. "One of Princeton's priorities is to make the program cost-neutral for families," says Scott Leroy, Associate Director of Princeton's Bridge Year Program. "Currently we're heading into our seventh cohort, which will offer the program to thirty-five students."

The Tufts program, which launched in 2015, offered its first fifteen spots to incoming Tufts students. For more than half of the participants, the program was completely free due to their financial aid packets. The program pays for all the needed airfare, health insurance, a living stipend, and an online course that aims to enrich the experience of students while they're abroad.

EARNING COLLEGE CREDIT

While it's rare that students are able to earn college credit for a gap program, it could be an avenue worth exploring with your teen.

But first, a warning: Rounds says you should consider the impact that earning college credits may have on the experience. Attending a gap program in the hopes of earning credits could limit the experience of the student. Plus, turning credits into something valuable after the gap may be a long shot.

"The programs that offer credits vary in quality. I always want to make sure that the credits are deeply relevant to the experience of the student. Being an educator, I would vet it like crazy because there's nothing worse than thinking you're escaping boring high school classes, but then you end up taking a poorly designed course that's asking you to 'click here if you're culturally sensitive,'" Rounds says.

He continues: "The last thing we want to do is communicate to a young person that you can have this profound experience, but then still have to take a course that's not at that level. This makes them wonder if that is what they have to look forward to in college. That would be a disincentive."

Still, with the right amount of upfront time and research, it is possible to make college credits for a gap year work. Rebecca Cruze's mom, Shelly, felt justified in using college money to fund a gap year because Rebecca earned thirteen credits on her trip to Thailand with Carpe Diem. To ensure those wouldn't be buried at the bottom of an electives list that didn't matter, she called the University of Oregon (where Rebecca was enrolled for the following year) and worked with the school to create a program of self-study that matched actual coursework to her daughter's experience.

Because Rebecca traveled through Southeast Asia and spent time learning Thai, she was able to fulfill a required freshman language course for three credits. She also earned credits for a philosophy class because she spent time exploring Buddhism and interviewing monks. "Along with college credit, it gave her focus for her travels and an opportunity to reflect through a daily journal," says Shelly.

Carpe Diem is one of the few programs that offers college credit for over thirty courses, including philosophy, religion, geography, geology, women's studies, history, and art. Their program is fully accredited through Portland State University, so students are able to use their financial aid—as determined by federal guidelines and the Free Application for Federal Student Aid (FAFSA)—to help pay for the gap year.

FAFSA support is often a combination of low-interest loans, grants, and scholarships. In the Carpe Diem program, students who go this route are expected to journal daily, participate in group discussions, interview locals, and write one to two essays when they return. "It's really a way to connect the dots between experiences," says Drew Edwards, the program's executive director.

If your child has been accepted to a university and is deferring, it's best to speak to the registrar as early as possible to ensure the credits from a program will transfer. If your student hasn't identified and applied to schools yet, it's still possible to transfer credits later, but be aware that it's a bit more of a gamble.

This exercise in deciphering whether college credits are a possibility is a good chance to give your child the opportunity to flex their independence muscle. Encourage them to call the office of the registrar to discuss their options instead of you doing it all for them.

GETTING CREATIVE

But what if you're really in a bind financially, your child doesn't qualify for aid, and the scholarships have all passed you by? It's still not a lost cause, and there are plenty of ways to fund a productive gap year.

If you're going through a program, dissect the outlined fee, then try to reduce it as much as possible. For example, matching gifts from companies and organizations in your neighborhood can help to support a gapper. In addition, Tomkin says some programs, like Cross-Cultural Solutions, are non-profits, which means participants can claim the experience as a tax deduction.

Another avenue that may be unpopular with some students, but a strong indicator of a successful year, is asking your child to contribute financially.

"I heavily advocate that the parent make the son or daughter contribute financially to the program no matter the family's level of affluence," says Ethan Knight.

Karl Haigler and Rae Nelson, authors of *The Gap-Year*

Advantage: Helping Your Child Benefit from Time Off Before or During College, agree: "Whether they're holding a bake sale, working over the summer, or paying for the whole thing, everyone we interviewed for our book said contributing financially to their experience added to what they took away from the gap year, including appreciation for budgeting and the value of education."

As a parent, Shelly Cruze says she felt strongly that Rebecca should have skin in the game for these same reasons: "It was important because it made her more serious about it. It's not a penalty, it's an empowerment, because as an adult, you have to pay for things. And I think it made it more special for her."

Shelly asked her daughter to fund 20% of the trip, an amount the family agreed was reasonable given Rebecca's savings. "We heavily subsidized it, and the grandparents also gave her money, so it was a big deal to have everyone participate so she could go do this," Shelly says.

So, what if your teen has no savings? How about some good, old-fashioned fundraising?

FUNDRAISING FOR THE GAP

Fundraising for themselves can help to teach kids

skills—such as determination, confidence, persua-sion, and initiative—before they head out for their gap year. Kids can organize community car washes, bake sales, or walk-a-thons to support their cause. They can approach the editor of the local newspaper and suggest an article about gap years in general and their gap year plan in particular, with a plug at the end about their fundraising campaign.

"We had one student who ice-skated through the canals of Camden, and people donated money for every mile. What a great experience to have on its own for leadership and organization," says Tomkin. "Traditional fundraising works. Everything from writing letters to two-hundred people who you have contact with, or posting on social media, to putting together a dinner and doing a little presentation." Your teen can also check out GoFundMe.com, IndieGoGo.com and Kickstarter.com, which provide a platform for raising money on social media.

Asking your child to pony up may also encourage them to incorporate the social and global issues of wherever they're going into their fundraising efforts. If they host a dinner or make a project that ties into the places they'll be visiting, it immediately connects them on a deeper level to their gap year experience.

GAP YEAR VERSUS
COLLEGE STUDY ABROAD

I didn't get my first passport until I was twenty-one. Our family vacations consisted mainly of drivable destinations, and though I occasionally tagged along with my grandparents to Canada, I never needed a passport for the places we traveled. That doesn't mean I didn't have a feverish travel bug lodged firmly inside of me, and I've since made up for lost time. My friends joke that I'm on a plane more than I'm in my apartment.

That desire to travel is why I was so excited to learn about study abroad when I started applying for colleges. I'd never even heard of a gap year, but I still couldn't wait to jet off to study somewhere fabulous and foreign. The admissions counselor and my advisor did a solid number selling me on the benefits of study abroad, and I ate it up. That is, until I took a hard look at the price tag. I was barely making my rent and paying my tuition. There was certainly no way I could afford the added cost of going overseas.

Shelly Cruze says she had a similar experience when she started evaluating study-abroad courses with her daughter. "I was shocked. If you've got your kid in an in-state program and then they want to study abroad, all of the sudden you're looking at a huge added cost.

It's a complete misconception that it's affordable, and the schools sell you a bill of goods a bit. I felt like in some respects, the gap year programs were cheaper than study abroad in college."

Shelly's impressions hold up. A *Forbes* article titled "Six Ways to Cut the Costs of Your Study-Abroad Program" found the average cost of a study-abroad semester is $31,270, or about double what a semester at private colleges costs. The cost of study abroad was cited as the single largest nonacademic deterrent to the program among students.

By comparison, most gap programs cost anywhere from $500 to $20,000, with extensive, heavily supervised nine-month programs, like the one offered by Winterline, topping out at around $50,000. For students doing independent gap years, costs vary based on location and activities.

Besides the fact that study-abroad programs cost a lot more, they really are no match for the experiential learning a gap year provides, according to Tuft's Mindy Nierenberg. "Study abroad is just that: study," she says. "Many people try to use it like a gap year, and they don't pay much attention to the courses that they're taking, which is detrimental to what they're supposed to be doing. If a student doesn't academically get out of it what they can, then they're wasting the experience and tuition dollars."

She adds that study-abroad programs rarely allow for any type of service or volunteering, and if they do, most schools don't grant credit for it. Her advice: "If you really want something that is experiential, then you should take a gap year."

ASK YOURSELF:

- Does my place of employment offer matching donations?

- Have I explored whether my local government organizations support gap years?

- Is it important to me that my child pay for a portion of the program him- or herself?

- What sort of fundraising possibilities might our family engage in?

ASK YOUR CHILD:

- What types of fundraising activities can you do to raise money?

- How do you feel about funding a portion of this year yourself?

- Have you narrowed down programs that interest you and offer tuition breaks?

- Have you filled out your portion of the FAFSA?

- Have you contacted the office of the registrar to ask about earning credits?

9: WEIRD, WACKY AND WONDERFUL...RIGHT?

"My father was expected to grow up playing an instrument really well, but his parents would never in a million years have allowed him to do it as a profession. It was drummed into him he had to be an engineer or do something where he could earn a steady paycheck. Play the violin in amateur orchestras, play for the family, but do not for a minute expect to earn a living at it."

–Tara Fass, Los Angeles family therapist

How many big dreams are dashed because they're "unrealistic?" When we ask young children what they want to be when they grow up, most of us smile and offer encouragement, even if the child says garbage truck driver or McDonald's burger flipper. While I'm not advocating for the career aspirations of a four-year-old, it's interesting to think about at what stage of life we start judging a child's answer.

Is it sixth grade? Ninth? Junior year? When—and more importantly, *why*—do we lose support for the weird and wacky? And when do kids start to tailor their answers less for themselves and more for the desired external response?

On one hand, I get it. It's hard to make a living in an established profession, much less an unstable one. For every successful artist there are hundreds, if not thousands, of starving artists. By limiting the pool of options to the tried-and-true, parents are trying to protect their children from making mistakes. But in fact, narrowing the choices could extinguish the passion.

Often parents have this myopic perspective that it has to be law, medicine, accounting, or a corporate profession, but the idea is to follow your child's lead as opposed to imposing your own. "So, if you look at your child and they really get excited and interested in superheroes, then okay! Great talents have emerged with love for superheroes," says psychologist Karen Bridbord.

In practice, this can be a hard sell for parents, but the result of parenting with restrictions on what career is acceptable can severely impinge on a child's sense of self. "When a child's feelings are dismissed, they are taught that what they think or feel is not important," says Bridbord. "They can start to doubt themselves, a pattern that can haunt them for life. With a sensitive child, there is a further vulnerability to becoming a caretaker to a parent's emotional life—that is, becoming responsible for regulating their parent's emotions. So when they feel like their parents are anxious by what they've said or done, they quickly retract and do or say something else. What happens over time, when that becomes a pattern, is that the child loses connection to themselves—to who and what they like and want."

As more and more Millennials enter adolescence and adulthood, these issues with self-awareness and self-doubt appear to be mounting. When a connection to the self isn't fostered, or parents are always stepping in to direct their child on how to behave, it can manifest into huge issues that go well beyond choosing a career. Because we can't isolate things, not encouraging kids to make decisions for themselves can result in their doubting their own likes and dislikes, and even being unable to choose a suitable life partner.

"People come to me and say, 'I really don't know what I want to do with my life,' and then I start probing, and it's not just about their careers. They have a hard time making decisions in general," Bridbord says. "For kids who come from homes where parents don't support their decision-making, every decision can become a source of pain and conflict."

As I touched on earlier, our whole lives are spent individuating. There's never an end to that process, because our whole lives are about becoming. But when a child has never been authorized or encouraged to think on his or her own, or when parents have checklisted out every activity on the road to college, then issues surface because the anxiety can feel never-ending.

"There's nothing inherently wrong with a checklist of things to be accomplished in order to set ourselves up well for the next thing in life; to be successful we have to set goals and work hard to reach them," Julie Lythcott-Haims writes in her book, *How to Raise an Adult.* "But if we've taught our kids that there is one predetermined checklist for their lives, we may be constructing a path that is more about us than them. And a path that isn't about them may be a path to nowhere."

Take the classic example of the musician: "That's their

passion, but how many end up in law school? I've met so many lawyers who end up only later exploring their passions. They didn't want to be a lawyer, but they were pressured. Or they felt like at least law was a good education that could prepare them for whatever they want to do later. In that way, law has become the next liberal arts education," Bridbord says.

In some cases, that person may become a musician later on, and may even credit law school for teaching them to think about the world in a different way. But for the person who doesn't ever get to their passion, they're denying themselves an authentic life, which can create trouble later on.

"When people work on something that they don't want to do for long periods of time, it can take a toll on their emotional lives. I've seen this lack of authenticity result in cynicism," says Bridbord. "They feel like they're not living their true self out, they're not actualizing who they are at the core and instead are working in a profession that they don't connect to, or that doesn't speak to who they are."

As you can imagine, that sense of inauthenticity can drum up negativity that can result in depression and anxiety. Bridbord says we spend more time at work than we do with our families and friends, so having to spend time in a job we hate—especially while we're passionate about something else—can be very painful.

If, as a parent, you're relating to this struggle, it's important to realize that the issue isn't in your child's aspirations but instead may lie with you. But you should also understand that it's not your fault. "Sometimes the parent never had an opportunity to choose their own destiny," says Bridbord. "They got sucked into their parents' vision, or never fully individuated themselves, so it can be extremely threatening to have your child do that. It can bring up jealousy for parents."

In my early twenties, I had a friend named Peter whose parents questioned his every move. When he relocated from his small town in Minnesota to Chicago, they told him he would fail. When Peter built up a success-ful freelance career as a graphic designer, his parents questioned why he didn't have a "real job." And when he fired all his clients to take on a full-time role at a multi-million dollar corporation, his dad told him to enjoy the company perks while they lasted because "it wasn't real life" until he was hating the daily commute and felt just as miserable as the rest of the workforce.

When I met Peter for lunch one day shortly after this

conversation with his father, he threw up his hands and said, "I've worked on both sides of the spectrum as a freelancer and a corporate, and nothing makes them happy. I can't win!" He went on to tell me that his mother and father were stuck in lives they found unfulfilling, and he'd come to realize that rather than applaud his persistence to find happiness in his life, they unconsciously chose to cut him down instead.

Peter's choices weren't the problem. The issue was his parents' unhappiness with their own lives that was manifesting into jealousy. Even though my friend understood that this was happening, it still didn't make it any less painful. Like all children, he still wanted their support and approval.

Situations like Peter's play out all the time with varying outcomes. In some instances, the child rises above and finds support elsewhere, perhaps in a teacher, therapist, or partner. But in other cases, children can atrophy and spiral off track, making it difficult for success down the line.

Because it's impossible to predict which way a child will go, it's critical to understand what's going on inside yourself so you can prevent this struggle within your child.

IT REALLY DOES TAKE A VILLAGE

Finding support and guidance can go a long way in overcoming your obstacles. Being a parent is stressful, and no one's expecting you to have it all figured out. "Parents are just human beings," says Bridbord. "But even the word 'parent' has this greater-than-life connotation, this responsibility."

For parents who are dealing with their own painful pasts and presents, it's difficult, if not impossible, to parent well in a silo. That's why it's so important to find additional support, especially during transitional times when stress levels are at an all-time high.

One option is to seek counseling to unearth what's at the root of your opposition. A good therapist won't only offer advice, but he or she can assist in getting you in touch with your feelings, which will put you in a better position to have similar conversations with your child.

If you're uncomfortable with the idea of seeking professional help, getting involved in community parenting groups, or at your child's school, can have a similar positive effect. The old adage "It takes a village to raise a child" certainly stands, and it's critical not to isolate yourself, because everyone has blind spots.

How do we manage this? How do we respond to our children who are navigating a world we didn't navigate? How do we make sense of it all?

These are all questions that a good parenting group or class seeks to answer. "Too often, parents think they're doing what's best when they're not. There are things we don't know we don't know," says Bridbord. "But the more we allow ourselves to be exposed to other ways of doing things, or to differing opinions, the more we grow and enhance our own parenting skills."

ASK YOURSELF:

- If I'm opposed to my child's plan, what is the reason?

- What's at the root of my concerns?

- Am I being honest with myself about my feelings?

- Can I identify what I'm feeling?

- Has my own sense of self been fostered?

ASK YOUR CHILD:

- If money, training, and time were no obstacle, what would you do with your life?

- What would you do if you knew you couldn't fail?

- How do you want to be remembered?

10: DEALING

DELICATELY WITH DEFERMENT

"Colleges are looking favorably at taking a gap year. A lot of parents think it hurts their child's chances to get into college, and that's just not true."

– Ethan Knight, AGA president

Nearly every family I spoke with told me there was never a question of whether their child would go to college after the gap year. In most cases, students applied to school, got accepted, and then deferred their enrollment.

Defer, defer, defer is Carlton Round's advice. Still, that doesn't mean the schools will always let you off easy. "The schools will say things like, 'I can't guarantee your financial aid packet next year.' Don't listen to them." Rounds has worked in academic administration for more than twenty years and has mentored his fair share of students through the deferral process. "They don't even know what your financial aid packet really is when they're telling you that. And they usually accommodate you, no matter what."

Mindy Nierenberg says that at Tufts you just need to let the admissions office know. "You just say you want to defer, and you can defer. You don't even have to give a reason." Some schools will say to let them know when you're applying and that it won't affect your chances of admission. Nierenberg says she's heard some administrators advise, "Don't tell them on your application, but let them know afterwards." She adds: "I don't think there are many schools that have a problem with you deferring after the fact. In the end, they want the student."

She does recommend letting the school know earlier rather than later. If a student doesn't let admissions know until July or August, it can be harder for a school to fill the spot with a waitlisted student.

TIPS FROM ADMISSIONS

Washington Post reporter Adrienne Wichard-Edds interviewed Parke Muth, a veteran college admissions consultant who spent nearly three decades at the University of Virginia. In an article titled, "Want to Help Kids Succeed in College? Let Them Take a Gap Year," Wichard-Edds quotes Muth as saying he advises that students interested in taking a gap year defer, but offers some words of wisdom about when and how: "Announcing that you'll be taking a gap year can sometimes come off as [sounding] overly privileged, like you can do anything you want and get your parents to pay for it." Muth suggests students should not mention deferment in their college applications and instead should request it after being accepted.

Reading this, you might assume that the process of deferral is simple: meet with the dean, fill out a form, and that's that. While that's the case for some schools, there are other schools that still have issues with deferral.

When Riley Wong applied to college and gained acceptance into multiple public and private schools, he found that some schools were less willing than others to grant his deferral request:

"UC Davis had some hoops to jump through, and while UCLA asked for more information about what he'd be doing, they ultimately said they supported gap years," says Riley's mom, Pia.

Round's advice? Put down multiple deposits in order to secure your spot. "The schools will say, 'Don't put down multiple deposits.' But for $200? Put down a few deposits because I guarantee the student is going to come back [from the gap year] saying, 'I want to reassess where I want to go.' How awesome that they come from a place of strength picking it this time, as opposed to being uninformed."

That's what happened with Riley, who ended up choosing UCLA. While Berkeley also allowed him to defer, Riley's gap experience made him rethink his major, and Berkeley didn't offer his new program of interest.

Perhaps schools are becoming more accepting of gap years because they're paying closer attention to how they can help fix social problems associated with adjustment and identity. These expensive issues, including switching majors multiple times and binge drinking, are running rampant on campuses today, and administrators everywhere are scrambling to find a solution.

THE FOUR-YEAR MYTH

Today only 19% of full-time, public school students earn a bachelor's degree in four years. Even at state flagship colleges, the number is only slightly better, with 36% of full-time students completing their bachelor's on time.

While more and more schools are being judged on whether they can get students through in four years, it's not proving to be an easy task. In a study of more than five hundred eighty public, four-year institutions, only fifty have on-time graduation rates at or above 50% for their full-time students.

So just how long does it take to earn a "four year" degree?

According to data from the U.S. Department of Education, for a student who starts their college studies at a four-year university, the average time it will take to graduate is *five years and eight months*. "That means students need to be even more judicious about what they do," says Rounds.

Taking a gap year isn't the answer to every problem that colleges face, but as we'll see in this chapter, when students can more clearly articulate *why* they're going to school, everyone wins.

A TELL-TALE EXAMPLE

Let's look at a common situation and break down some costs:

Mark graduates at the top of his class, which opens him up to a wide selection of colleges. He chooses to attend a public university in his home state, where yearly tuition hovers just above $15,000. If he'd gone to a public college out-of-state, his tuition would be nearly $23,000. And had he chosen a private university, he'd be paying upwards of $37,000 or more per year.

He goes in "undecided" and fills his schedule with general-requirement courses. By the middle of his freshman year, Mark decides to declare a major in marketing and starts taking courses to fulfill the prerequisites.

Things are going pretty well until halfway through his sophomore year when he meets an alumni working in international aid. Suddenly, he realizes marketing doesn't make his heart sing, so he ditches that idea and recalibrates his schedule accordingly. Mark's not alone. In fact, 75% of students switch majors at least once in college.

In the worst-case scenario, Mark may add an additional year or more onto his expected graduation date, which means he'll pay a full extra year of tuition, *plus* any lost wages, since he's not out in the workforce. Research indicates he can expect to tack on an additional $68,153 to get his paws on his bachelor's degree. But let's not assume the worst-case scenario and only look at the extra cost of the individual courses. If most of Mark's marketing credits transfer to his new major, and he's only taken five courses—or fifteen credits— that he doesn't need, that's not too bad, right? It may not seem like it, until we start doing the math.

At his school, a credit hour costs roughly $440, so in taking five courses, he's spent an additional $6,600. That doesn't account for any of his time in class, the added stress of the course, the materials and books he purchased, or the time he wasted studying for tests and doing homework that could have been better spent elsewhere.

When we calculate in the average cost of these factors, Mark's swap takes a toll: he's spent nearly $8,900 *for just five unneeded courses.* Five courses isn't uncommon: on average, students going after a bachelor's degree will take fourteen to fifteen extra credits.

If Mark had needed to change schools, as nearly 60% of all bachelor's recipients do, he could have lost even more credit hours. Shockingly, nearly half of all transfer students lose some or all of their credits.

The sadder story is that Mark will probably graduate with his new degree, give it a shot in the real world, and realize it's not what he expected. Unfortunately, the education system isn't designed to expose students to their career choice in action until it's too late to realistically alter their journey. Again, he's not alone. Only 27% of college grads have a job related to their major.

At the end of the day, colleges are big business, and contrary to our idealistic view of the service they provide, they're not set up to help a student "figure it out." On average, there's one advisor assigned to every four hundred students on campus, which means overwhelmed students with no clear direction are making uninformed choices that lead to costly and timely mistakes.

The truth is that students aren't getting the help they need on college campuses. And even if good help is available, many of them are too consumed in making new friends, worrying about classes, and—yes, partying—to really make a college career center work for them.

"When they're at the university level, most students

don't even know that a career counseling center exists," says Bridbord. "If they do know about them, they often don't feel comfortable seeking them out. Additionally, the resources that exist in public schools are abysmal, and the student/counselor ratio is ridiculous. How can students possibly get the kind of care and attention they need to help them figure this out?"

In many ways, a gap year can frontload these issues by giving the student a chance to explore and experiment without the pressure of grades, the stress of tuition, and the strong pull of social commitments.

In a study of more than seven hundred students who took a gap year, 98% report their experience helped them to develop as a person and allowed time for reflection, while 97% claim increased maturity and self-confidence. All of these outcomes better align students with a clear purpose for attending college after the gap year.

MATURATION, MALES, AND PARTYING

While a gap year can benefit nearly everyone, Rounds says he wishes males, in particular, were forced to go. He gives two reasons. First, men's first-year drop-out rates are double that of women's. Second, males are "more culturally isolated, and they're rewarded for certain behaviors that slow maturity," explains Rounds. "Men are very underrepresented, particularly in the private colleges, and are less academically prepared as students because they are always a little behind the curve to begin with. That's why I think it's extra important for them to go international."

He adds: "The irony is when they develop broader and more mature skills, their grades go up, and because they're men, they end up getting privileged in the liberal arts system because they're so underrepresented."

This claim that men may benefit more than women from a gap year was also explored in The NY Times article, "In Fervent Support of the Gap Year." Due to the maturation that inevitably occurs during a gap year, Bob Clagett, former Dean of Admissions at Middlebury College, is quoted in the article saying, "If colleges encouraged more male students to take a gap year, it would reduce a lot of the alcohol-related problems on campus."

Currently, national statistics report that four out of five college students binge drink, and about 25% of college students report academic consequences of their drinking, including missing class, falling behind, doing poorly on exams or papers, and receiving lower grades.

Again, a gap year may help solve this problem—at least in part. Surveys and informal conversations with students who take a gap year indicate that gap year kids typically drink and party less than their counterparts who go straight through college following high school graduation. Susan H. Greenberg, author of *The NY Times* article mentioned above, says this about her daughter's gap year:

"As a bonus, taking time off seems to have inured her to the binge drinking so rampant among new freshmen. When you've spent a year legally sipping pilsner with intrepid friends in European pubs, hanging out in a dorm room doing shots until you puke looks pretty unappealing."

Nierenberg says colleges are also paying close attention to how a gap year can help to positively affect the campus climate. "So many campuses are dealing with issues of binge drinking, or lack of compassion and understanding for each other, and those who come from different backgrounds. The thinking is that the gap year can contribute to changing that landscape, and we're going to be doing extensive research on this."

ASK YOURSELF:

- Have I considered the additional cost if my child doesn't really know what they want to study?

- Have I educated myself on how long it may take my child to earn a four-year degree?

- How might meaningful time off position my child for success in college?

ASK YOUR CHILD:

- Why do you want to attend college right now?

- Do you feel prepared and focused to make the most of college?

- Are you feeling burnt out on formalized education?

- How would you feel about starting college a year later than your friends?

11: FLY AWAY, LITTLE BIRD

"I am not a helicopter parent. I want my kids to go out and live life. Check in with me now and again so I know you're not injured or in trouble, but go have experiences. If we go a couple weeks without any word, I'm not worried at that point. I think it's better for a child to not touch base too much."

Rob Spach, gap year dad

During a gap year, parents and students can expect to feel some of the highest highs and lowest lows. On both sides, this can be an incredibly difficult experience, and as a parent, you may at times feel powerless, lack information, or have a yearning to set off on an adventure of your own.

Regardless of how you're feeling, when you speak to your son or daughter, try to keep the focus on their experience. Your child is in a foreign environment with new people, new challenges, and new stressors.

"If they have a really bad day, mom and dad might get an email where they're just venting and complaining. That's one of the hardest emails for a parent to receive when their child is on a gap year," says Drew Edwards, who's spent plenty of time on both sides of the parent/student divide. "But then three days later, they get an email: 'This is the greatest experience of my life.'"

Emotions tend to run to extremes, but when they run low, a student may resort to what's most comfortable. Especially in the first few weeks of the program, that comfort might lie not with a new leader who's supposed to be their mentor. "It's going to be mom and dad," says Edwards. "Parents need to know and expect that."

Due to the intensity of the situation, parents should expect some magnification or exaggeration. Rounds says a gap year is so intense because it's physical, mental, emotional, and political all at once. "Rarely [in everyday living] do you get to do all of that at the same time," he points out.

Since this may be the first time your child is

experiencing so much freedom and a very fast period of personal growth, they could at first lean on you heavily, or have the totally opposite response. Often, they're so pre-occupied with what they are doing that their emails to you sound short and distant. Something like, "This is awesome! Hope you're well!" is not uncommon. In this situation, you may feel very disconnected from the experience, but keep in mind that they're writing little because they're enjoying what they're engaged in.

THEIR EXPERIENCE, NOT YOURS

To some extent, the gap year is a family experience. You're preparing with your child, having discussions, and setting expectations about the time away. Once your child leaves, however, the experience becomes much less about your involvement. This can be difficult to accept, but it's also a stepping stone—perhaps the first real one—to your child becoming a full-fledged adult.

Dynamy runs a parents' day twice a year where administrators spend time talking with parents about the scaffolding approach I spoke of earlier. "We tell parents that if they crowd their kids when they're trying to grow, then they don't have that space to grow," says

Kathy Cheng. "So what we ask parents to do is take a step back. And then, wherever they think that step is, we tell them to take two or three more steps."

When Pia Wong's son Riley decided to take a gap year in South America before going to college at UCLA, she was all for it. Travel and exposure had always been important aspects of their family's dynamics, and Riley was burnt out from years of sports, clubs, and academics in high school.

Once he was gone, though, she says the hardest part was her inability to communicate with him whenever she wanted. It didn't help that Riley's group was terrible at keeping their blog updated the way the other groups did.

"That was really hard. I missed him. I worried about him. I wanted to know more about his experience. But really, it provided a turning point for me as a parent. I thought, 'This is the first experience he's having that's completely his.' He was doing things that the rest of the family hadn't done, going to places that no one else had visited."

Pia says that while this was a little sad because she didn't get to share in her son's adventure, it also made her realize how important it was for Riley to have his own time to grow. "After all, it's only going to continue to happen more and more as he gets older, which is a good thing," she adds.

Ethan Knight, President of the AGA, agrees that taking a back seat during a gap year is one of the greatest things parents can do: "The experience is for the student, and it's about them coming to terms with what they want to do with the rest of their life. It's about who they are, and doing that with their parents hovering can be a real hindrance to exploring themselves as individuals." He doesn't advocate for cutting your son or daughter off entirely, but rather allowing your child to dictate their own terms for how they relate to you.

LEFT BEHIND AT HOME

Shelly Cruze was another parent who worried at home while her daughter Rebecca went off on a gap semester to Thailand. She says she joked with her friends that she felt like a jilted lover: "I was always wondering, 'Will I see a picture of her? Will I hear from her?' You just hang on everything while they're gone."

Shelly said Rebecca was really good at writing letters and keeping her up-to-date, but it was still strange not knowing when her daughter would check in. "She would just show up online, or I'd get an email. And it was at odd times—in the middle of the night, or I'd be at the gym and I'd drop everything. We were only able to Skype once, but that was just amazing. I was so happy to see her."

Just like Pia Wong, Shelly came to realize that this was her child's experience, and as a parent, she had to let go: "They're going to do what they're going to do, and they're going to have this experience, and you're not going to be thrilled about everything that goes down."

When college isn't the right fit, having a child in school can be even more painful than the lack of contact during a gap year. Rob Spach's son Christopher attended his freshman year of college but was unhappy. "The truth of the matter is that he really didn't want to go to college in the first place," says Rob, a college chaplain in North Carolina. "Education is very important to our family, so we really urged him to go onto college and try it. He didn't want to go, but he also didn't even know a gap year was a possibility."

Once Christopher learned about the gap year, he jumped at the chance to take a break between his freshman and sophomore years, and his parents were eager to support him. After his gap year, Christopher re-enrolled in school with an adjusted major, and his dad says he has a new perspective on college that didn't exist before his time away. "Seeing his unhappiness was more of a challenge than being out of touch with him when he was in Nicaragua and Scotland," says Rob.

CULTURE SHOCK, IDENTITY, AND HOMESICKNESS

Just like in the transition to college, some students adapt quickly to a gap year, while others take more time to settle in and get their bearings. As a parent, it can be hard to watch your child struggle to adjust, but Rounds says most people fall into a standard spectrum of emotions when confronted with issues like culture shock.

There are students who go on a gap year and have very little initial reaction to the culture. They don't experience culture shock, and they don't go through a "honeymoon period." For those people, says Rounds, the experience slowly amps up during their time away. On the other hand, there are times when students arrive and are immediately hit with intense culture shock, causing them to struggle for the first few days or weeks. "I always let people know that both of those scenarios are completely normal," he adds.

Because students come from various subgroups, they may also have different sets of needs that influence how they adjust. Rounds says because he works with diverse racial and socioeconomic backgrounds, different questions come up for various students about how they'll be accepted by the group.

"We can also group sexual orientation and gender identity into this conversation because often, quite frankly, they're a group that has access to resources but are so uninvited in general because they or their parents are afraid they're going to be bullied," explains Rounds.

He says for parents of children who've come out, the instinct may be to not send them into an environment where a parent can't control the outcome: "If you can't control the environment, they could be in danger. True, but that assumes here at home they are kept safe and are not in danger," he points out. "Sometimes the students who get protected because of perceived vulnerability already have advanced coping and resiliency skills. These, when translated in-country, often propel them to excel beyond their peers."

Along with questions of identity and the culture shock of being in a country that's vastly different from home, issues of homesickness are also common. In general, there are two types of homesickness. There's homesickness that students get over, and there's homesickness where they're anxious and not ready to be away.

The former kind of homesickness is the most common issue gap year students face, and luckily, it's fairly easy to regulate. "A student may need to make a friend, or talk to the group leader, and they get over it. It's just that kind of 'Holy smokes! This is really different here,'" says the AGA's Sarah Persha.

Let's assume your child has this relatively benign type of homesickness, and not the more serious anxiety issues we discussed earlier. As a parent, what's the best way to comfort a homesick kid who may be thousands of miles away?

Persha says you should never tell your child to "just get over it" or tell them "it will get better." A better option is to engage your child in a meaningful conversation, which can relax them. "Ask your child to tell you something that had meaning for them in the past few days, and to tell you something that was hard for them," Persha advises. "That way, they can think of something that they visually, auditorily, or tactilely were involved with the day before." She says it's important to focus on duality in the conversation—both the good and the challenging parts—because that acts as engagement and calms the child's brain down. "Even if they're eighteen-year-olds, they're still kids. This approach is also helpful because as humans, when we retell a story, our breathing actually calms down and our psyche relaxes."

Something else that can be hard to manage is remaining neutral while your child is pouring their heart out about how much they miss you. Persha says it's vital that you not attach yourself to whether your child stays or goes. "I teach parents to say, 'Gosh, I'm sorry to hear you're feeling homesick. Tell me more about the experience so far.' If their child pushes them to let them come home, I usually tell the parent to say, 'Before I would even think about making such a decision, I would want to know that you are actually talking to the leaders and some of the other students about your feelings.'"

The reason for this is because by remaining neutral, you're triangulating yourself with your child and the experience. The greatest mistake parents make in this situation, says Persha, is aligning with their child instead of inviting him or her to be more mature: "This is an opportunity to talk through solutions about what the student can do about these feelings, or who they think they can talk to." Again, this is why—even if your son or daughter is doing an independent year—it's so important to have someone on the ground in their environment to act as a main point of contact in moments of distress and loneliness.

IN CASE OF EMERGENCY

Occasionally an emergency arises that needs to be dealt with immediately. In these scenarios, the best programs are well-equipped to deal with anything that may arise—a broken bone, a stolen vehicle, a lost student, or some type of political unrest or natural disaster.

Good programs also take great care in choosing group leaders to ensure they have the medical training necessary to stabilize a situation. "All of our leaders are wilderness first responders who have a high level of medical know-how," says Drew Edwards.

Reputable programs will also have a comprehensive plan in place that establishes very clearly how you'll find out if something goes wrong. Edwards says the Carpe Diem philosophy is to keep parents apprised of every situation, and depending on the specific emergency, to contact them hourly or daily to monitor progress.

Still, not everything that appears to be an emergency actually is one. Sometimes dependent or homesick students may not respect the difference between a true emergency and an excuse to call home: "We do a lot around defining what is and is not an emergency at the beginning of a program. Is it that the library is closed in a foreign country? Because if your mom calls, she can't help you with the country's library. But if you lost your meds, then that's a different story," Rounds says.

Students may go to one extreme or the other when it comes to reporting problems. On one hand, they may not alert the staff because their pattern is to hide issues for fear of getting in trouble. On the other hand, there are students who won't go to anyone except their parent because that's the dynamic of their relationship. By discussing in advance what constitutes an emergency and how problematic situations should be handled, you can prepare your child in advance to handle difficulties, should they arise, appropriately.

SETTING EXPECTATIONS AND TONE

An amazing opportunity exists before your child leaves on a gap year to set the tone for the year—and for the next stage of your relationship. "So often kids are told, 'This is what is right or wrong, do this, don't do that.'

That's not what a gap year is about," says Edwards.

To start, look over the program materials or the rules you've outlined as a family, and invite questions based on what's included. For example, you might say something like, "Hey, Sean, I know you drank a few times in high school, and there's going to be social pressure to drink on this trip. How are you going to feel if you're presented with that situation? Are you at all nervous about it?"

Creating an open and honest conversation around such topics allows you to begin breaking down the barriers between you and your child—and puts you on a playing field that's closer to equal. "Conversations like these set the tone for empowering the student to make the right decisions. There's such a difference in a kid when they're told what the right decision is versus when they come to it on their own," Edwards says.

ASK YOURSELF:

- How am I preparing to take a backseat during my child's gap year experience?

- Have I put parameters in place to allow my child some breathing room?

- Have I spoken with my partner about how to react if

our child calls in distress?

ASK YOUR CHILD:

- Do you know who to talk to within the program if a problem develops?

- How are you feeling about being away from the family for so long?

12: RALLYING THE

SQUAD FOR RE-ENTRY

"I think the knee-jerk reaction is to throw a big party and invite all the neighbors to show the student how much they were missed. But often, the student needs a bit of space to process the experience and work through some of the challenges that are associated with their transition back."

– Scott Leroy, Associate Director, Princeton's Bridge Year Program

Parents should be prepared to welcome a different child back into their lives after the gap year. Even though it's exciting to witness growth and drastic change in your child, it can also be slightly nerve-wracking waiting for him or her to return.

"One of the biggest issues is the kids who do a gap year feel changed, and they go back to their hometown and they think, 'Wow, something is different. My friends did a year of college and they seem the same, but I feel like I'm breathing different oxygen now,'" says Persha.

An often undervalued part of the gap year is transitioning back in with friends and family who've been on a different trajectory. Fundamentally, what your child values in life may differ—even from your own views—after their time away. "Think about it as before gap year, it was pop culture, fitting in, and making money. Students get back from their gap and now they find interest in fellow humans, the welfare of society, and living a life with purpose and meaning," says Ethan Knight.

This shift can be tough to handle, especially because the student may want to talk about the experience much more than people want to listen. It's possible everyone around them will get sick of hearing about their gap year very quickly.

As a parent, it can be exhausting to constantly act engaged if this is the only topic your child wants to discuss. Expect for them to share inside jokes as if you should understand, and be aware that there are parts of the experience that are beyond words. Above all else, keeping an open mind and being willing to hear about the experience for extended periods of time can go a long way in making your child feel comfortable.

"It's incredible to be able to listen to your child, and be someone who they can share this with. Try to cultivate a curiosity about your kid, which I don't think we always do as parents. We tend to think we know everything about them," says Mindy Nierenberg.

Re-entry can be one of the most challenging times in the gap year process, and your child needs a strong support system because they may start to feel lost. Keep in mind that not only gappers who travel abroad go through the shock of re-entry.

In programs such as Dynamy's Internship Year, teens stay in the States, but re-entry can still be a hurdle: "For our students, the issue is often around going into post-secondary and running into institutional life. That's an adjustment because they feel like Dynamy was so amazing and supportive, and then all of the sudden they have to deal with someone like a registrar if there's a problem," says Fred Kaelin, Dynamy's executive director.

Lucy Buckman did travel abroad, and she says the return home after the first part of her gap year was very difficult. Though she had high school friends who had also done gap years, they had joined programs while Lucy did an independent year, volunteering in Peru and studying Spanish.

"I had a hard time relating to my friends because I felt like I had all these different experiences in Peru, and I was losing that by leaving the country. Going home, I had no one to talk to about it," Lucy explains. "Because my other friends had similar experiences through a program, and my experience was much different than theirs, it was almost even harder to relate to them about it."

She says keeping in touch with her fellow volunteers and her homestay family in Peru helped, as did talking with people who were genuinely interested in her experiences back at home. "Most people asked, 'How was your trip?' And I'd say, 'Great.' And then that was it. I felt like I had all these experiences worth sharing, but my few-word answer sufficed for them."

To kick-start meaningful discussion about the trip, ask pointed questions to draw out stories and experiences that your child wants to share but might not know how to. A good opportunity to create an environment for questions is to have your son or daughter walk you through their photos. As you view the pictures, ask things like "What was happening here?" instead of questions with just yes-or-no answers, such as "Did you have a good time?" "Ideally, students in programs have been engaging in these in-depth ways of talking and listening, so for parents to be able to pick up on that and meet them there will really soften their landing," says Edwards.

That your child may come back with new ways of communicating is something you should be aware of. Cleveland teacher Daniel Gray-Kontar's students sometimes feel confused about how the things they're learning in the classroom fit into their very different outside lives. "They'll say, 'We are learning about philosophy and meditation in this class, but there are people in our lives who are not afforded the luxury of understanding these concepts. So it makes us feel a little weird, because we're getting stuff that a lot of our peers or parents are not. So, what do we do?'"

If your child comes back communicating in a different way, or talking about concepts that are unfamiliar to you, Gray-Kontar says the best thing you can do is to listen and attempt to learn from them: "I know that's difficult for parents to do because we watch our children do some really boneheaded things. But we're all in states of becoming, all the time. And even when we're adults, you know what? We're still sometimes doing some boneheaded things."

Gray-Kontar observes how if we have a friend who is going through a tough time, most of us will show support, compassion, and understanding, even if we know the friend is making a mistake. We may say things like, "He's having a hard time, and he's just not getting it. But I'm his friend, and I'm going to stick around for him."

"That's the same thing you have to do with your child," says Gray-Kontar. "Your child is also always in a state of becoming, just like that friend is. They're really not very much different. They're just younger, and they're in your house all the time. But they deserve that same care, compassion, and understanding, and we should allow them to make mistakes, but still understand that they have a lot to offer."

FIRST WORLD PROBLEMS

If the gap year involved a developing country, parents can also expect a bit of disdain from their kids for the amount of opulence or waste in America. Try to keep in mind that they've lived in a very different way for the last few months. "They've actively had conversations around food deserts and water scarcity, and have been taking cold-bucket showers and loving it," says Edwards. "It can be a very jarring experience to come back in. Parents should be super aware of that, and very patient."

When Riley came back from his time away, his family says he wasn't really into bathing. "We kept thinking, 'When will he cut his hair?' laughs his mom. "The program had prepared us for that, and we appreciated it. Water is precious."

Another important aspect of re-entry is continued reflection. "If not reflected upon, a gap year can come off as wanderlust and not very educational. Make sure you help your child to translate the experience into college and potential careers down the road," advises Knight.

Once your child is in college, he or she may feel much more mature than the other incoming freshman. Not only are they older because they've deferred, but they also feel a bit alien, based on their experience. Persha says the best thing to do in this situation is to encourage them to find significant people to connect with: "They're going to feel different, more mature, more exposed, worldly, so make sure that they get involved in a club, whether it's language or an aid society for the country they visited. Something that can help them stay connected to that elevated, expanded place that they went to."

If there's not an organization that speaks to their interests, Nierenberg recommends you encourage your child to launch a club of their own. Even starting a club that connects them with other people who've done a gap year can be a good way to get them interacting with like-minded students.

At Princeton, Scott Leroy says this tightknit network of gappers has been one of the most powerful outcomes of the Bridge Year Program. "When freshmen come in after their experience, they're immediately welcomed by bridge year alumni who are sophomores, juniors, and seniors. They've created this really dynamic and interesting network, whereby they don't necessarily form a cohesive club or group but they remain close and connected. There's a great mentorship that occurs between upperclassmen and freshmen, and these kids have an incredibly rich community that they're tapped into on day one."

Seeking out online communities can also be a good

way to form a bond with others who have had a similar experience. Until recently, there haven't been many places for gappers to connect online. Alumni networks run by programs vary in activity, though Thinking Beyond Borders keeps a list of past gappers who blog about their experiences.

To help with re-entry transition and beyond, I've also launched the first global community of gappers called "Gap to Great." It's a place where students can connect with one another to share stories, swap photos, and offer advice. There's also the opportunity to get in front of employers who value and understand the gap year experience. You can find it at www.gaptogreat.com, or on my website in the Gap Year Resource section.

YOUR CHILD ON CAMPUS

Aside from helping your child find a community to engage with, work with them to connect the skills and knowledge they've acquired with the courses they're taking. "A gap year gives students a higher level of learning and of understanding things," says Nierenberg. She tells about a student who took a public health class after her gap year and ended up studying an issue she'd seen posters for every day while on assignment at a clinic overseas.

You can also expect your child to have a deeper understanding of the impact that their actions have on other people. "Take a student who trashes their residence hall," Nierenberg says, by way of example. "Someone who's been on a gap year where they've had to live in a community understands more how their behavior has an effect on their neighbors. They're not as self-centered as the average first-year student."

Across the board, administrators and professors say gap students generally have greater leadership abilities, don't hang back, and are ready to jump in and get things done. Leroy says he's been surprised by the willingness of gap year students to take major chances. In more than one instance, he's seen students return from gap years who walked onto varsity sports teams at Princeton. One teen, who had never wrestled a day in his life before his gap year, found a passion for traditional Indian wrestling during his time away. As a freshman on campus, he walked into varsity wrestling tryouts and convinced the coach to take a chance on him.

"It's also true in the coursework," says Leroy. "Bridge year students aren't as daunted by the idea of enrolling in a class that's completely unrelated to their major because they have this curiosity. They're less concerned about how it might affect their GPA and more willing to put themselves out there and try something different."

As a parent, you can nudge along these tendencies by exposing your student to options they may not be aware of. For example, if your child did a gap in a culturally rich place like Mexico and took an interest in the arts, ask them, Nierenberg suggests, if they're familiar with majors like Latin Art History. This can help open their eyes to the range of possibilities in college.

A NEW KIND OF RELATIONSHIP

In terms of managing the bond with your enlightened child, much of it will depend on your relationship before your son or daughter left. But that doesn't mean this isn't a brilliant opportunity to shift the dynamics of your interactions.

Often kids can feel trapped into behaving a certain way around their parents because those are the expectations and habits that have formed around the relationship. Typically, there's a renegotiation that naturally occurs when a student returns from a gap year, regarding the student's lifestyle.

"What the student values and prioritizes has evolved a

lot during this time. On the other side, the parent has an expectation of the relationship that may not really meet the new reality, so there's a process of re-establishing relationships," says Leroy. "My advice is—to whatever extent possible—have fewer expectations in terms of what your son or daughter will be like when they come back."

This transitional time is stressful, but it's also ripe with opportunities to right the ship. I know for me, even a small window of time away from home did wonders for my relationship with my parents. I think if most families are honest, they will tell you absence really does make the heart grow fonder.

If the time away has brought up realizations or emotions for you or your child, re-entry is a good time to nurture your relationship as it moves into the next stage of life. For example, perhaps your child really struggled to adjust without you, and you realize you've enabled a dependency in them.

"My advice is to start where you are now," says Tara Fass, a family therapist in Los Angeles. "You have to start trusting them, and you have to develop tolerance to let them fall and pick themselves back up, to really learn from their mistakes and suffer consequences.

I think the hardest thing for parents is standing by while their child makes mistakes and finds their way."

Psychologist Karen Bridbord agrees. "Maybe the last eighteen years haven't been what you'd hoped they'd be, but start where you are. And start with, 'I'm sorry, and I'm trying.' That's a great way to begin the discussion." If these are conversations that might come up, know that it won't be easy, but they will do wonders for your relationship from this point on. For many parents, admitting things have been rocky can be painful, but it's imperative if you're trying to mend a ruptured relationship.

Bridbord offers more advice to jumpstart the healing process: "When you do mess up or make a mistake with your children, it's okay. Being able to go to them and say, 'I'm sorry. I made a mistake. And here's what I meant to say or do,' teaches your child such an invaluable lesson at that moment of taking responsibility and not being defensive. If only parents did that, there would be a possibility of healing wounds. That would be a gift. And parents don't realize that no matter what stage of life it is, they can give that gift to their kids."

ASK YOURSELF:

- What am I most curious about in terms of my child's experience?

- Am I allowing the space my child needs to continue to share?

- Am I asking questions that engage my child?

- Am I being honest about the state of our relationship?

- Do I feel comfortable saying "sorry," if that's needed?

ASK YOUR CHILD:

- How did you feel when you encountered that situation?

- Tell me about a time during your adventure when you felt really alive.

- What was a moment where you were really uncertain of what to do next?

- Have you thought about it this way?

- Have you considered a major in that field?

- Did you know this option was a possibility?

13: AVOIDING

THE POST-GRAD SAD

"To foster creativity and innovation in our youth, let's keep our expectations very high. If we raise the expectations we have of young people, they will always meet them. They will not only meet the challenge, but they will be even more creative."

– Daniel Gray-Kontar, TEDx speaker and Cleveland school teacher

Almost 90% of America's workforce is not able to contribute their full potential because they don't have passion for their work. How depressing is that? Say what you will about passion in the workforce, but life is certainly easier when you enjoy getting out of bed in the morning. In the case of gap year students, many say their experiences helped them land a little closer to their ideal career, and while plenty of gappers will inevitably shift focus and recalibrate before they've "made it," at least they're getting a head-start in the right direction.

We've already looked at how gappers benefit in college, but is it possible their experience will also translate into the workplace? The answer is a resounding yes. Time away to focus on something that's exciting and fulfilling could be exactly what an employer is looking for. Mindy Nierenberg tells the story of a neuroscience major, and what landed her a job in finance and fundraising at MIT. "When she graduated, she decided to take a year off to work on a fishing boat in Alaska, something she'd always been interested in. Then she came back and did something related to her major and realized it wasn't what she wanted to do, so she applied for the MIT position."

Nierenberg says she asked the girl, "What in the world do you think made them choose your application? There must have been so many people with backgrounds in finance!" The young lady answered: "I know! The person who interviewed me said, 'Anyone who would go on a fishing boat in Alaska must be an interesting person. We care about the whole person, and we don't just want people with a set of skills that match, we want people who are independent and creative.'"

Her interest and passion—not just her degree—led to her landing the job. It shouldn't be surprising that employers are paying attention to the skills students learn during time away from higher education. U.K. studies on the effects of a gap year on employability found that during a well-planned break from formal education, "participants gain a wide range of life skills and other more specialized skills. These are often the ones employers identify as lacking in new recruits and are valued by universities."

Think back to the first chapter. The soft skills employers find valuable align perfectly with the core competencies that researchers Karl Haigler and Rae Nelson identified in gappers. Leadership, adaptation and coping, working well with others, and taking initiative in decision-making are all proven skills gained during a productive gap year.

So employers are happy when they're getting candidates who have these skills, but what about the employees? Are they satisfied when they're finally getting that new job?

STOPPING THE MILLENNIAL TURNOVER

It seems that everywhere you turn these days, you find an employer complaining about Millennial turnover. In 2014, an *Atlantic* article reporting on the issue said: "At PricewaterhouseCoopers, the accounting giant, the employee exodus became so pronounced that executives commissioned a companywide investigation in 2013 to figure out what was happening." So, what did they come up with?

Ninety-one percent of Millennials (compared with 71% of Boomers) insisted that achieving career success is necessary to living a good life. Also in higher percentages than past generations, they valued a good life/ work balance, quality time with family and friends, and achieving personal goals and dreams. As I mentioned early on, the Millennials' mindset of blending work with life (and life with work) is at odds with the current system of work in America, which unsurprisingly leads Millennials to search for greener pastures.

But even with all the hype about Millennials leaving jobs, you may be shocked to learn that they're not doing so at a faster rate than their parents did. In fact, data from the U.S. Department of Labor for 2014 exactly matches 1983 data on the average tenure for young workers aged 25-34. It only seems like a higher percentage of employees are jumping ship because there are now over 53 million Millennial workers in the labor force.

In the first quarter of 2015, Millennials surpassed Generation X to become the largest share of the American workforce—and data indicates that their numbers are highly likely to continue growing. By 2020, 40% of the American workforce will be Millennials. By 2030, that number will jump to 75%.

When you start crunching the numbers, it's easy to understand why professionals are banging their heads trying to figure out ways to keep Millennials on the job. On average, it costs $15,000 to $25,000 to replace a Millennial. When you consider that Millennials are moving jobs every eighteen months, you start to see why this is a dilemma. If a company of a hundred people employs eighty Millennials, they're spending anywhere between $900,000 and $1.5 million in turnover costs. At a national level, $11 billion are lost annually due to employee turnover, and employers spend $72 billion on employee recruitment every year. Not a pretty picture.

But how can employers keep Millennials around for

longer than eighteen months? They can start by hiring for "cultural fit," which is another way of saying that a person's core values align with that of the company's. There are several reasons for doing this, but two of the biggest are that employees who "fit" stick around longer, leading to fewer costly turnovers. When the right employees are in the right roles, high-turnover organizations report 25% lower turnover, and low-turnover organizations report 65% lower turnover. Employees hired for fit are also more engaged with their work, which contributes to more job satisfaction and a higher return on investment for the company.

When we consider the numbers, along with the fact that companies with engaged employees have twice the productivity of companies without them, it's not hard to see why employers may want to examine candidates' reasons for applying before hiring them.

Unfortunately for employers, even if they do everything right, including hiring for cultural fit and keeping employees engaged, it's still not all rainbows and sunshine. Studies show that even engaged employees will eventually move on. So what's a company to do? A study from the auditing firm Deloitte found that "while workers who are merely engaged won't actively seek to achieve higher performance levels to the benefit of self and firm, passionate workers will."

These "passionate explorers," as the study refers to them, are defined by how they respond to challenges: "Do they get excited by, and actively seek out, challenges? How do they solve problems? How do they learn, develop skills, and build their careers over the long term? How do they interact with others to pursue those goals? Through their behaviors, explorers help themselves and the companies they work for develop the capabilities to constantly learn and improve performance. Rather than a one-time performance bump [as in the case of merely engaged employees], explorers deliver sustained and significant performance improvement over time."

The qualities that identify a passionate worker align perfectly with what we know gap years help to cultivate: problem-solving abilities, enthusiasm for challenges, the ability to work in a group to pursue a common goal, and the unrelenting curiosity for learning and exploration.

PUTTING SCIENCE TO WORK AT WORK

In essence, this values match and the Millennial mindset is driven by one key factor: purpose. When we boil down what passionate Millennial workers are asking for, it looks roughly like this: "How does the work I'm doing serve my greater purpose for being on this earth?"

For the past three years, Arthur Woods and his team have been hard at work trying to help employees find positive answers to that question. Woods is the co-founder of Imperative, a business focused on helping companies find and support purpose-oriented workers, and helping purpose-oriented workers find meaningful jobs, where they can bring purpose to work every day. Imperative's goal is to put technology and real science around how we measure purpose in the workplace.

What he's discovered so far is that purpose has three elements: (1) why we do what we do, (2) what drives and intrinsically fulfills us, and (3) how much meaning and fulfillment we experience. By getting to the heart of why someone works—either for a paycheck, a promotion, or a purpose—Woods' diagnostic has allowed Imperative to help people create a formula for purpose based on identification of: "Why am I working? What drives me? And how much purpose am I experiencing?"

Bridbord says that when she thinks about purpose, passion, and employee engagement, the financial world comes to mind as an example of what happens when purpose and passion are ignored. "Because I'm in New York, I end up seeing a lot of people in that world, and I've never met a person in finance who was really happy with what they're doing. They're making lots of money, but still they have a feeling of emptiness."

The truth of the matter is that money, as research shows, is not what makes people happy. There's no question that when you are unable to pay your rent or buy food that you will be unhappy, even if you're doing something that you love. But the acquisition of wealth is by no means predictive of satisfaction and happiness. Employers understand this, and as Millennials with altruistic career aspirations start flooding the workplace, companies are getting hip to hiring on core values instead of sky-high expense accounts.

But if students don't know what makes them happy because they've been running at full speed on our social treadmill, it's impossible for them to identify their passion, which in turn, makes it difficult to for them to add a high level of value to an organization.

Again, it all comes back to self-awareness. Consider that a gap year is an opportunity for your child to become more self-aware, so they will be able to find out what they love to do. "What a great gift to be able to give your child," says Bridbord.

WHERE INNOVATION COMES FROM

So let's say we've got a set of passionate, engaged employees who were hired for cultural fit. They're cranking out work like champions, but now leadership wants them to take it up a notch. It's time to innovate. After all, the most successful and sustainable companies are the ones able to stay relevant, creative, and innovative. Want to know the number-one quality that sparks innovation? *Exposure to obscure and unrelated experiences.*

When we peel back the layers on some of the most creative thinkers, an interesting picture begins to emerge. Creativity and innovation come from the ability to make associations between seemingly unconnected things. Remember the story of the guy who invented Netflix? One day, while picking up his mail, his mind linked two unconnected things: the nuisance of having to go to a store to rent movies, and the ease of picking up the mail. Presto: the concept of mailed movies was born.

Another example is Steve Jobs, who used his experience taking a random, one-off calligraphy class to help him design the first Apple computer. Jobs is quoted as saying, "None of this calligraphy had even a hope of any practical application in my life. But ten years later when we were designing the first Macintosh computer, it all came back to me. And we designed it all into the Mac. It was the first computer with beautiful typography. If I had never dropped in on that single course in college, the Mac would have never had multiple typefaces or proportionally spaced fonts."

According to Harvard research, this is called "associating," and it's the number-one skill that separates innovators from non-creatives. In *Iconoclast: A Neuroscientist Reveals How to Think Differently*, author Gregory Berns writes, "To see things differently than other people, the most effective solution is to bombard the brain with things it has never encountered before."

What better way to bombard the brain with new experiences than a gap year? And before you say, "Ah! But Jobs learned that *in college*, not out traveling the world," Berns also notes that epiphanies rarely occur in familiar surroundings. In fact, when we look at Jobs' innovative life, as author Carmine Gallo does in *The Innovation Secrets of Steve Jobs*, we notice a pattern: Jobs had a very winding, experiential life that included everything from a few college courses, to studying the intricacies of Japanese rice-making appliances, to reflective meditation retreats in Indian ashrams.

Universities can't teach creativity, and yet creativity is what's needed to solve problems, says Neil Campbell, author of the book *Innovated Thinking: It's Time to Liberate Yourself.* He argues that education has been institutionalized with "the embedding of concepts (beliefs, behavioral norms) within defined, 'accepted' frameworks." But in order to solve the problems of the future, we need to raise adults who are capable of doing new things, not blindly follow in other generations' footsteps.

The problem doesn't lie in human nature. It lies in how we rear our children. Kids are innately creative—they don't get bored, and their imagination allows them to have fun in any situation. "We train them away from that for security and protection, and eventually we kill this creativeness. But that creativeness is needed to solve problems. So by the time they get to high school and you ask them what they want to do, the answer is, in short: 'I don't know,'" says Campbell.

Teacher Daniel Gray-Kontar adds that in order to facilitate creativity and innovation, we should keep an element of play in our daily lives: "With teens and adults, we forget the importance of play, and we forget that so much learning comes from playing. We should be encouraging and continuing to reinforce the importance of playing in teenage and adult years. Out of playing, you get so much creativity."

Students competing in the mad race for college have been stripped of so many essentials that create innovative and curious learners, capable of changing the world. Don't you think it's time we pumped the brakes and seriously evaluated who we're helping? When we zoom out on the bigger picture of where our current systems are leading us, the scary answer is: no one.

IF COLLEGE ISN'T IN THE CARDS

Much of this book has been about making the jump to college after the gap, but what if your child is in the 10% of students who don't go back to school after their gap year experience? There's still plenty to suggest they can use the gap to their advantage.

"When you look at our society, there are certain stamps of approval when you get a college degree," says Bridbord. "But the reality is that there are many people who never graduated college who became extremely successful because they were so passionate and driven to do what they wanted to do." If the goal in life isn't only to check the boxes, but to actually make a difference and be happy, then highly motivated people can be successful regardless of whether or not they earn a degree.

Perhaps most importantly, we should remember that a college degree is by no means indicative of future happiness, even in the case of "successful" people. "There are highly successful people who are not satisfied because they have the ability to do things like get through medical school, but never really feel fulfilled and rewarded by their work," Bridbord says.

In the case of the student who doesn't go to college, a gap year could provide the fire to finally go after their passion, better identify their purpose, or lead them to discover a path where they can flourish and thrive. As we've seen, in the quest for creativity, unexpected experiences can trigger whole new ways of being and unlock the potential for more than we initially thought possible.

HOW TO FRAME THE GAP EXPERIENCE

Gap year researcher Karl Haigler, former Special Advisor to the Governor for Literacy in Mississippi, spent time traveling through Belize when he was in college in the late 1960s. When he returned to the U.S., he took an interest in international relations, going so far as to conduct political and sociological research.

"I wrote a paper based on the research, which was something government agencies ended up being very interested in," Haigler says. "That proved the value of the gap year to me, and it also allowed me the opportunity to do things in the intelligence field and international relations. That experience really helped me in terms of my career."

As his scenario suggests, the experiences of a gap year can be framed in a way that catches the attention of an employer. But it's not as simple as saying, "I took a gap year." Many employers may not know what that even means, so it's up to the student to present the information clearly.

"Before they talk to an employer, they need to do some brainstorming about the skills and knowledge they've gained during their gap year, and think about translating that into skills that transfer to the job market. Then, [they need to] put those into their resume in an appropriate way," says Nierenberg. For example, if your daughter created a library for donations in a small town, then in her resume she could include skills involving organization, management, and an understanding of community education.

If the student is in school, Nierenberg recommends that they meet with the college's career-counseling center to determine the best way to translate the gap experience into something useful: "It's free, and the student can take a list to them so they can figure out how to put it on a resume." If your teen isn't getting the service they need at a center, or if they're not in school, there are near-infinite resources you can find online to help with resume development.

ASK YOURSELF:

- Will I allow my son or daughter the opportunity to find their wings?

- Do I believe that experiences are the backbone of innovation?

- Am I cultivating a culture of curiosity in my child?

- Am I holding onto my own ideas of what my child's future should look like?

- Am I assisting in my child's individuation or hampering it?

ASK YOUR CHILD:

- What career resources are available to you on

campus or in the real world?

- How do you feel your life experiences can translate to the workplace?

- How can you use the gap year to your advantage?

A CLOSING MESSAGE

Looking past the gap year and the college years, time off is not something our culture does well. In America, more than half of us don't even take our paid vacation time. Unsurprisingly, that's not a good thing. "Overworked people tend to burn out, produce lower-quality output, provide lower levels of customer service, become depressed, and sometimes just flail around in their exhaustion," according to the report by Deloitte. "Giving people time off lets them relax, engage, and perform better."

Smart companies such as Google build in policies that force employees to take time off. They call it 20% time—a day a week that's set aside to work on something new or outside the normal job function. If innovative employers realize that we humans need a break to function at our highest potential, I can only hope that more and more universities, educators, and families will start to draw the correlation between burn-out in the workforce and burn-out among students.

In the end, I believe that the Harvard degree hanging in a corner office isn't the symbol of the next generation's American dream. My generation and the generation of those who come after me want something more. We want the promise of change, we yearn to make a difference, and we want to soak up every ounce of life. Never before has the world been so accessible to so many, and while that causes a whole new set of problems, we feel like we need to go out and experience them firsthand before we can attempt to solve them. We want to secure not just our paycheck, but our purpose.

From my generation to yours, I'm asking you to give us that chance. To analyze the driving forces in our society that are pushing us to the brink of exhaustion and apathy. To identify our personal values and passions, through innovations like the gap year, so we can steer a course through the future that aligns with who we are. We want to work, we just want to do it on our own terms.

I'm asking you to recognize that those terms are probably different than yours. They're probably different from what you thought we'd be seeking, which I under-stand can be off-putting. At the same time, please realize that they're not any less valid. While it can be a scary proposition to go against the grain and opt to stand out from the crowd, I truly believe the health of our planet, our communities, and our children rests in our ability to do just that.

So, will you give us the chance?

ACKNOWLEDGEMENTS

I never knew what topic I'd choose to write about for my first book. Now that it's done, I realize that, in some ways, a writer doesn't choose which book to write, but rather, the book chooses the writer.

Thank you to the gap year community, especially Ethan Knight and Drew Edwards, for inspiring me with your determination to make the world a better place for students everywhere. You are fighting the good fight, and I feel honored to stand alongside you on the field.

Thank you to Karla Sanders, my beautiful, brilliant, and patient designer who made creating this cover a highlight of the publishing process. Thanks to my editors, Jessi Rita Hoffman and Meredith Whitney. Your keen eyes kept me from completely putting my foot in my mouth on multiple occasions.

A huge thanks to the KPI team, and especially to my writing mentor, Andrew Griffiths, who pushed me to challenge myself and get sh*t done.

And last, but certainly not least, thank you to my family for their support and encouragement. I wouldn't be the woman I am today without your (sometimes tough) love. This one's for you.

ABOUT ANDREA WIEN

Andrea is a Millennial, entrepreneur, and writer. In 2015, she launched the first global gap year community, Gap to Great, as a place for students to share stories, ask questions and provide support for one another before and after the gap year. She's the founder of Aviator, a personal development program focused on creating connections and opportunities for young adults.

Her weekly column on *Forbes* chronicles the future of work, and the ups-and-downs of launching a business. Her writing has appeared around the web for publications including *USA Today, Yahoo!, Thrillist, The Huffington Post* and *Seattle Weekly.*

On Andrea's podcast, also called Gap to Great, she interviews people about their obstacles, successes and non-traditional life paths.

Though Andrea didn't take a gap year, she likes to say she's taken many gaps in her years. Born and raised in Northeast Ohio, she's lived in New York City; Seattle, Washington; and Sydney, Australia since graduating in 2007 from Ohio University with a bachelor's degree in journalism and public relations.

She currently lives with her husband in New York City.

CONNECT WITH ANDREA

For a list of resources mentioned in this book, go to andreawien.com/gapyears.

To book Andrea for a speaking engagement, send an email to events@andreawien.com.

To connect with Gap to Great, Andrea's online community for gappers, go to gaptogreat.com.

You can learn more about Aviator at onaviator.com.

Podcast: andreawien.com/podcast

Website: andreawien.com

Email: a@andreawien.com

Twitter: @AndreaRenee

CPSIA information can be obtained at www.ICGtesting.com
Printed in the USA
BVOW02s0736070516

447189BV00005B/170/P